EDITOR
Susan E. Laemmle

MANAGING EDITOR
Hara E. Person

BOOK REVIEW EDITOR
Laurence Edwards

POETRY EDITOR
Adam Fisher

EDITORIAL BOARD
Alan Berlin, Jonathan M. Brown, Paul Citrin, Benjamin David,
Andrea Goldstein, Paul J. Golomb, Karyn Kedar, Richard Levy,
Dalia Marx, Michael Shire, David E. Stern, Michael A. White

PRODUCTION
Publishing Synthesis, Ltd.

COPY EDITOR
Michael Isralewitz

CCAR ELECTED OFFICERS
Ellen Weinberg Dreyfus, President
Jonathan Stein, Vice President
William I. Kuhn, Financial Secretary
Richard A. Block, Treasurer
Debra J. Robbins, Recording Secretary
Shira Stern, Membership Secretary

CCAR RABBINIC STAFF
Steven A. Fox, Executive Vice President
Deborah Prinz, Director of Program and Mentor Services
Lennard Thal, Interim Director of Placement
Hara E. Person, Publisher and Director of CCAR Press

Arnold I. Sher, Director of Placement Emeritus (1989–2008)
and Interim Executive Vice President (2005)
Paul J. Menitoff, Executive Vice President Emeritus (1994–2005)

PAST EDITORS
Abraham J. Klausner * (1953–58), Joseph Klein* (1958–64),
Daniel Jeremy Silver* (1964–72), Joseph R. Narot* (1972–75),
Bernard Martin* (1975–81), Samuel E. Karff (1981–84),
Samuel M. Stahl (1984–90), Lawrence Englander (1990–93),
Henry Bamberger (1993–96), Rifat Sonsino (1996–2000)
Stephen Pearce (2000–2003), Jonathan A. Stein (2003–2009)

*Deceased

CCAR Journal
The Reform Jewish Quarterly

Symposium Issue on Politics and Spirituality: Rabbinic Dilemmas

Contents

FROM THE EDITOR
At the Gates — בשערים 1

ARTICLES
ESTABLISHING A FOUNDATION

Politics: A Prophetic Call to Rabbis 3
Richard N. Levy

Not Your Father's (or Your Mother's) Advocacy: The Moral
 Voice of the Rabbi in Challenging Times 12
Marla J. Feldman

Ritual Versus Justice: Must We Choose? 25
Suzanne Singer

Dissent from the Dissenters 31
Clifford E. Librach

WHEN RABBIS TAKE POSITIONS
Principles of Rabbinic Advocacy

Same-Gender Marriages from the Intersection of
 Faith and Politics................................. 46
Arthur Gross Schaefer and Robert Cornwall

The Ballot, the Bimah, and the Tax Code 58
Ellen P. Aprill

Liberal Dilemma: The Prophetic Mandate versus Religion-State Separation in Reform Political Discourse 72
A. Brian Stoller

Examples of Rabbinic Advocacy

Rabbis for Obama: The Role of Rabbinic Leadership in the 2008 Presidential Campaign 99
Samuel N. Gordon

Rabbis for Obama: A Rabbi for Obama 107
Steven Bob

Scariest Night 112
Jerrold Goldstein

It Wasn't a Giant Leap but a Natural Next Step 120
Allen I. Freehling

WHEN CONGREGATIONS TAKE POSITIONS
The Jewish Case for Community Organizing

Power Precedes Program: Relationships and Politics in the Pulpit 126
Larry Bach

Where the Sanctuary and the Public Square Meet: The Story of Temple Israel's "Vote No on One" Campaign 133
Stephanie D. Kolin

POETRY

For Yaakov Ari Ringler 151
Stanley Chyet z"l

Shofar 153
Debra R. Hachen

BOOK REVIEWS

Just Torah—A Review Essay 155
   Whose Torah? A Concise Guide to Progressive Judaism
      Rebecca T. Alpert
   Righteous Indignation: A Jewish Call for Justice
      edited by Or N. Rose, Jo Ellen Green Kaiser, and
      Margie Klein
Reviewed by Eric Caplan

Drawing in the Dust 162
Zoë Klein
Reviewed by Pamela Wax

*From Rebel to Rabbi: Reclaiming Jesus and the Making
   of Modern Jewish Culture* 166
Matthew Hoffman
Reviewed by David Fox Sandmel

Join the Conversation!

Subscribe Now.

Engage with ideas about Judaism and Jewish life through essays, poetry and book reviews by leading scholars, rabbis, and thinkers.

A Journal for All Jews
The CCAR Journal: The Reform Jewish Quarterly
$75 for one year subscription
$125 for two year subscription

For more information and to order, go to:
www.ccarpress.org or call 212-972-3636 x243
CCAR | 355 Lexington Avenue | New York, NY 10017

At the Gates — בִּשְׁעָרִים

The origin of this symposium issue goes back to an e-mail message sent out by Steven (Simcha) Bob and Samuel Gordon on November 7, 2008, to colleagues who had joined onto Rabbis for Obama. The message thanked participants for efforts that had contributed to Barack Obama's Election Day victory. That very day, shortly before Shabbat, I replied to Simcha and Sam from my new position as editor-elect of the *CCAR Journal*, suggesting that they write an article on their organizing experience—an article in which they would step back from that specific set of circumstances to develop some general ideas about the relationship between Judaism, especially rabbis, and politics.

Sam's draft article reached me on November 15 and sat in my "Ideas for the *Journal*" file for a while. In February 2009, the *Journal*'s editorial board supported the notion of a symposium issue with the working title "Rabbis and Politics." By then, I'd had enough experience to know that the element crucial to this issue's success was the choice of a guest editor. Thankfully, Richard Levy came to mind.

In thinking of Richard and then persuading him to accept, I called upon our longstanding relationship. Before becoming my boss in Hillel work, Richard had been the person who suggested that I, an academic in my early forties, become a rabbi. Richard's talents as a liturgist, writer, Reform Movement leader, and counselor are well known; his background as someone who cares deeply about spiritually driven political action, less so. It was the combination of these qualities that commended Richard to me and that in the end probably led him to accept the guest-editing invitation. They shine forth in the articles you are about to encounter—directly, in Richard's introductory piece, "Politics: A Prophetic Call to Rabbis," and indirectly in the work of other authors, who responded to the Call for Papers or were enlisted by Richard.

Among the beauties of this issue is the way in which the authors, in effect, dialogue with one another. Without having read one another's pieces, they debate and disagree, and not only about the appropriateness of creating or joining Rabbis for Obama. It's not easy to press difficult, controversial issues without becoming acrimonious, but it seems to me that this symposium issue manages to do so in the best *eilu v'eilu* tradition. I believe this was enabled by the way in which Richard conceptualized the issue, changing its title to "Politics and Spirituality: Rabbinic Dilemmas," as well as by his capacity and reputation for fairness and generosity.

Our times challenge rabbis to fulfill a wide range of functions and expectations. We need all the help we can get in sorting them out and setting our own course. In no aspect of our work can such help be more, well, helpful than that related to politics. The *Journal*'s editorial board joins me in wishing you fruitful reading. We will be eager to get your reactions.

This issue is enhanced by book reviews and poems. Let the opening and concluding stanzas of "For Yaakov Ari Ringler" by the late, beloved Stanley Chyet serve as its epigraph:

> Jacob
> it's a time of noise
> a time of shriekings and stammering
> you come to now
>
> roar, Jacob
> give your meaning
> to this time

Susan Laemmle, Editor

Establishing a Foundation

Politics: A Prophetic Call to Rabbis

Richard N. Levy

On the last Shabbat in October 2010, an election year in the United States, rabbis across North America will be endorsing a candidate for public office from the pulpit. Not only will they be advocating for his selection, they will be invoking God's blessing upon it, and the chances are very good that every congregation across America will respond, "Amen!"

How can this be? In this volume of the *CCAR Journal*, dedicated at the inspiration of our editor Susan Laemmle to a multifaceted consideration of the role of the rabbi in issues generally deemed political, we have articles by Arthur Gross Schaefer and Dr. Robert Cornwall and by Ellen Aprill suggesting guidelines for rabbinic endorsements of issues from the pulpit. They both affirm that issues are fine but personalities are not, though they note that when the issues are endorsed by people who are running for office, the lines become murky.

But on Shabbat *Chayei Sarah* this fall—and every fall—any rabbi who reads the haftarah from I Kings 1:1–31 will be endorsing the selection of Solomon over Adonijah to succeed the dying David as king. And of course the haftarah will be introduced and concluded by blessings, praising the God who chose good prophets—like Nathan in this section who endorses the choice of Solomon—

RICHARD N. LEVY (C64) is rabbi of the Synagogue and director of Spiritual Growth at the Los Angeles campus of Hebrew Union College. A past president of the CCAR and former director of the Rabbinical School at the LA campus, he was the regional Hillel director in Los Angeles for many years. He is the author of *A Vision of Holiness: The Future of Reform Judaism,* published in 2005 by the URJ Press, and is the editor and chief contributor to *On Wings of Awe,* a High Holy Day *machzor* published in 1985 by KTAV, which will appear in a revised edition this year.

and found favor in their words. What could be more blatantly political?

You may object that this is not the same as advocating for a candidate in the 2010 election—this is at best an historical endorsement, after all. It is one thing to read an endorsement of one claimant to an ancient office over another and quite a different matter to lend one's name to a claimant for that office in our own time. The rabbi is merely reading a text, not, like our colleagues Sam Gordon and Simcha Bob, endorsing a contemporary candidate.

But is that the only difference? Why was it all right in the twelfth century B.C.E. for religious leaders to endorse a ruler, but it is not all right in the twenty-first century C.E.? One obvious difference is that there are no more prophets like Nathan to speak the word of God authoritatively to kings. But when the Rabbis decided to append the reading of prophetic texts to parashiyot in the Torah, they wanted to affirm that the truth of Torah did not end with the closing of Deuteronomy, but continued into the subsequent ages of Israelite history. Indeed, we can often detect how the Rabbis understood the relevance of the Torah in their own day by consulting the prophetic reading. Abraham's determination to continue the line begun in the womb of his recently buried wife is seen as an archetype of David's determination, with Nathan and Bathsheba's assistance, to continue his own line as well, a line that Jewish tradition has affirmed will be reestablished in the messianic time.

When we read this haftarah, we generally see it as a study of the courage of the prophets, of the inheritance of David and all he had meant and would mean for the people Israel, for the career of Solomon and his legacy (e.g., the Temple, the *m'gillot* he reputedly authored that we read on Pesach and Sukkot, etc.). We see it as a continuation of the lesson throughout the historical books about the accomplishments and the pitfalls, the moral highs and lows, of the monarchy. We do not see it as a political tract—and yet we could. And if we did, would that mean we should not read it on the October Shabbat before a national election? Would that mean we should cast it from the canon because politics has no place in the pulpit?

What do the words "politics" and "political" mean? The Oxford English Dictionary defines the former as "the science and art of government" and the latter as "of, belonging, or pertaining to the state or body of citizens, its government and policy." But the OED also acknowledges that "politics" can denote "political actions or practices, frequently negative." It is this last definition into which we have too often bought, rather than looking at the religious dimension of politics, which for Jews can begin with the model of God as *melech*.

I for one believe that there are few issues, few causes, that are purely "political." Can discoursing about a war be "political," when it occupies so much space in the Torah—from Genesis 14, to the wars Israel is asked to fight in the wilderness, to the laws of war in Deuteronomy 20, to the descriptions of wars in the historical books, to Maimonides' expansions of the laws of war in the *Mishneh Torah*? Brian Stoller argues that by using the categories of *hilchot milchamah* Reform Jews "bring the values and teachings of a particular religious tradition" into the secular sphere, and he provides summaries of several theories of political liberalism to argue that when we enter the secular realm as religious teachers we are jeopardizing our historic defense of the separation of "church and state."

Often we prefer the phrase "social justice" to "politics." One could argue that the goal of politics is to arrive at a just society, though some people fear that "social justice" is only ameliorative and does not aim at the radical (from "root") transformation of society that should be the meaning of the phrase *tikkun olam*, an expression that has come to suggest only incremental "fixings" rather than a wholesale "repair." Suzanne Singer argues that a concern for social justice permeates much of Jewish observance, suggesting that when we observe Shabbat or kashrut we are spreading justice in the human and natural spheres. In so doing she reminds us of a hundred-year-old dispute in the Reform Movement, viz., whether we can really separate "ethical" mitzvot from "ceremonial" ones. In the twenty-first century many of us have finally come to understand that just as God did not make such distinctions, neither should we.

But a similar issue arises when we discuss "politics." Issues of war aside, is the subject of health care "political" in OED's "negative" sense? Is it not primarily an extension of the mitzvah implied in *rapo y'rapei* (Exod. 21:19)? Is immigration "political" for a people who has wandered the earth for so many centuries and for whom *pidyon sh'vuyim* is also a mitzvah? Is concern for the earth "political," after decades of educational campaigns by Jewish environmental organizations should have shown us how deeply rooted (an appropriate metaphor) is concern for the earth in biblical and rabbinic literature—as well as in Zionist ideology?

One of the problems, of course, is that issues of war and health care and immigration and climate change cannot be significantly dealt with without negotiations by those who practice the "science and art of government," namely lobbyists and "politicians," from which comes the negative connotations of the word. But the *Chayei Sarah* haftarah demonstrates that political negotiations are a necessary part of fulfilling God's plan—and that, within the confines of the laws of this country, we must sometimes find a way to endorse a political figure to help effect that plan. (We now know that had the voters in Massachusetts endorsed a different senatorial candidate, the cause of health care would probably have been much better served.) Adonijah, of course, is the "bad guy"—but since Adonijah was David's oldest son once Absalom had been killed, he felt he had a claim on the throne, and in the political limbo that seems to have prevailed once David took sick, he may even have thought he was furthering the stability of the state and securing the Davidic line against possible usurpers. Besides, without him, David might have died without a timely designation of whom the king wished to succeed him. The point is that the players in this political drama seemed to be acting with the usual mixture of self-interest and altruism—concerned for their own legacy and for the longevity of the state.

It is important to view political dramas in our own time in the same way. While we often impugn the worst possible motives to players in the party or faction we oppose, as rabbis we need to step back and look for the best possible motives on each side so we can help our people make appropriate ethical and moral judgments in keeping with Jewish principles. Cliff Librach urges us to be wary of marginalizing those who dissent from the "majority" view in the Reform political sphere. While in the privacy of our own houses we are entitled to the same jaundiced view as anyone else; when we speak or act publicly as rabbis it is important that we remember that the will of God is carried out by flawed human beings struggling to perceive what constitutes right and justice. (If we believe these human beings are acting unjustly, of course, we have a right to say so.) It is instructive every so often to re-read Samuel and Kings to remind ourselves of all the "politics" in the Bible. Even the people whom it identifies as "good" engage in machinations to achieve aims that are intended to fulfill the will of God. Neither Elijah, Elisha, Gad, nor Nathan turn their backs on this politicking, but confront their kings on a daily basis. Nathan, after all, is the man who upbraided David for placing Bathsheba's husband in the line of fire. If we are to act in the political sphere as prophets, Nathan may be a better guide for us than outside scolds like Amos and Isaiah.

This of course raises the question as to what we mean by "prophetic Judaism" in the early decades of the twenty-first century. The prophets we generally set up as models are indeed Amos and Isaiah—and Jeremiah and Micah and the rest of the literary fraternity. But the authors of this symposium posit at least two different kinds of prophetic action: On the one hand, the individual rabbi who risks life and pulpit by traveling into the heart of a conflict (see Jerry Goldstein's piece on his involvement in the St. Augustine, Florida, demonstrations with Martin Luther King Jr.) or who becomes a professional problem-solver in city government (see the article by Allen Freehling, a kind of modern Nathan figure, on his new rabbinic role in Los Angeles.). On the other hand, we include two pieces (by Larry Bach and Stephanie Kolin) on the role of the rabbi who agitates a congregation from within to become a force for social change in the larger community. In a sense these two sets of essays demonstrate the tension between two views of what "prophetic Judaism" means today.

Those of us who went South in the 1960s—or who stood up for civil rights in their Southern pulpits in the 1960s—were in the model of the prophets who gave their names to books of stirring sermons out of the mouth of God to a sinning nation. Some of us faced much opposition from our congregations—our Southern colleagues faced death threats—but it was important to these rabbis that they fulfilled God's words to Isaiah (43:10): "*Atem aidai,* you are My witnesses." In this model too are all the rabbis whose sermons against injustice thundered from North American pulpits from the 1920s through the 1960s (see Marla Feldman's piece on the changes in rabbinic social justice from her childhood to the present). Their sermons did the prophets proud—and perhaps asking the extent to which they motivated their people to act is the wrong question. Like the rabbis who went and stayed in the South, these prophetic preachers saw themselves as witnesses—God needed to know that the people of God were made aware of the shameful conditions of working people, of blacks, of a nation reeling beneath the yoke of the Vietnam War, of the suffering Jews in the Soviet Union. The prophetic rabbi's role was to bear witness; now it was on the conscience of his (for most of that period) listeners to respond to the call.

For the past twenty to thirty years, fiery sermons have been rare in North American pulpits. As Suzanne Singer notes, the growing trend toward greater observance and spirituality for a while threatened to mute much of the prophetic agenda. As the community began to turn in on itself in the 1970s after the growing awareness of the full horror of the Holocaust and the shock of the Yom Kippur War, there was less appetite for social issues pertaining to the wider community. Furthermore, as the euphoria about Israel after the Six-Day War began to fracture into doubts about the right course for the State to follow in its pursuit of peace with the Palestinians, laypeople did not want the rabbi to force them to take sides between doves and hawks, and so group discussions of the Torah portion gradually started to edge out sermons that drew on the Torah portion to point the way for awareness and, ideally, action. In the process, sermons shrank in length—the half-hour sermon became rarer and rarer, often relegated only to the High Holy Days. The late Israel Bettan's legendary words came true: "If you don't strike oil after twenty minutes, stop boring."

The place of the sermon was taken by the Social Action Committee, and perhaps also by the Religious Action Center, whose resources and reach were far greater than any rabbi or congregation could muster. A good social action program was often a trip to the RAC, where members returned home inspired not only by the actions they could take, but by how much action was taking place in their name. *Atem aidai* had moved to the halls of power themselves—but the rabbis back home were seldom the witnesses.

The prophetic sermon remains an endangered species, if not actually a *goses*. But it need not be. An isolated sermon will not have any effect beyond bearing witness—but a sermon as part of an organized campaign can be very powerful. If yoked to the organizing techniques we are learning from Jonah Pesner's Just Congregations Department of the URJ, the sermon can regain some of its historic power—and the preacher can do more than bear witness, she or he can create a momentum for change.

The movement for faith-based community organizing is teaching us a great many things. The articles by Larry Bach and Stephanie Kolin discuss a lot of them. But an additional lesson it is teaching us is to reevaluate the nature of Reform as a prophetic movement—and to look at ourselves as a political movement. If the prophetic preachers were in the mode of Amos and Isaiah, the rabbis and others who do community organizing are more in the mode of Nathan, who work within a community of power day in and day out and influence the wielders of power by their relationships—as Nathan shows so effectively in the *Chayei Sarah* haftarah. "Community of power," you may ask? Since when is a synagogue or a Hillel foundation a community of power? There is power in numbers, in membership, in proximity, the organizers teach us. If a synagogue can turn out one hundred people to an "action" confronting a political figure for change, that is power. If three synagogues and three churches can turn out five hundred people, that is power that needs to be listened to. As the organizers remind us, "politics" is rooted in the Greek word "polis," the city-state, the home of the body politic. Politics in its ideal is enabling the body politic to speak to those who wield power over it and to remind them that in a democracy it is the body politic that bestows power and can also take it away. The Bible doesn't know from democracy, but it does believe that those in power need to follow the will of God. Synagogue-based community organizing sees itself as the communal bearer of *atem aidai*—bearing witness not as a rabbi to a congregation, but as a congregation, or community of congregations, to those in power, saying something like, "We are bearing witness to what our study and our faith lead us to believe God wants this community to do; how will you respond?"

Rabbis who do community organizing in their synagogues are building communities within their walls but also communities that will reach out to like-minded congregations. Yet rabbis engaged in this endeavor need not forsake the more traditional work of rabbis in a pulpit (preaching is harder for colleagues in Hillel foundations). But as organizers they know that the sermon cannot stand alone. Like Nathan, they know that the sermon comes out of their relationship with the congregation—see Nathan's rebuke to David over Bathsheba and his counsel regarding the succession. A sermon needs to begin in one-on-one conversations, where people share with the rabbi the concerns that "keep them up at night." As the rabbi begins to see common threads in these conversations, he or she can meet with groups of people who share similar ideas—indeed she or he might be developing several sermons at the same time, depending on the issues that are agitating the members. By convening "house meetings," some of the ideas in the one-on-ones can be crystallized, and groups can be set to work assisting the rabbi in doing the necessary research to make compelling arguments and share moving stories. Once these topics have energized all these people, the rabbi can strategize how the sermon can have its most forceful effect: Should he or she write pieces in bulletins leading up to the delivery date announcing the sermon and introducing the issue? Should there be opportunities after the sermon for its hearers to meet with members to discuss plans to act on various parts of it? A sermon so well prepared for can indeed be more than twenty minutes, for it will become a major focal point of the worship year. But it needs to be well written. It needs to be forceful, uplifting, based in text and Jewish ideas, so that it flows out of the service, out of the week's *parashah* or the festival season. It needs to be prepared, to be worked over, critiqued in advance, and delivered with reason and passion—in the midst of a service of prayer to God. It needs to address the prophet's critique:

> Don't keep bringing Me lying offerings,
> Incense is a foreign abomination to Me!
> Rosh Chodesh and Shabbat, convoking convocations—
> I can't stand iniquity at the concluding feast!
> When you spread your hands in prayer
> I will hide My eyes from you—
> Even if you pile up your prayers I will not listen—
> Your hands are full of blood! (Isa. 1:13, 15)

We need to say: We're not doing this, God. We're trying to call out for justice, to pass a bill for health care or equal marriage or immigration reform—and we're doing this in the midst of our prayers. We're trying to lift our calls for justice on the sounds of our prayers, we're trying not to speed through our prayers so we can get to the sermon, we're trying to offer You our mouths in prayer and our hands and feet in doing justice. This is what a prophet like Nathan, speaking at the climax of his work to educate and organize and uplift, means by "politics"—and it is what we should mean as well.

If we let our members bludgeon us with the slogan, "No politics from the pulpit," our heritage as a prophetic movement is doomed. If we can join the work that our colleagues are teaching us in organizing communities dedicated to social transformation, we can teach our members that politics is indeed an art—a moral and spiritual art: it is the means through which we can carry the mitzvot and other mandates of our tradition into the public sphere, not to coerce the government, but to make a cogent, faith-based case for change.

If indeed our heritage as a prophetic movement is under siege, let us work to redeem it, to bring the prophets back into our synagogue, to walk with them into the streets and into the halls of government. Sarah is dead, King David is dying, but a new generation is waiting to be born. We are that generation, and buoyed by Torah and the wisdom of Solomon, we can be worthy of those who have gone before us.

This issue of the *Journal* can help show us the way.

Not Your Father's (or Your Mother's) Advocacy: The Moral Voice of the Rabbi in Challenging Times

Marla J. Feldman

As I was growing up in Toledo, Ohio, in a classical Reform congregation, my earliest rabbinical role model was Rabbi Leon Feuer, z"l, who served our typical Midwest congregation for over fifty years. He was a classic—a stern, pulpit-thumping orator, whose booming voice berated and extolled, challenged and provoked those of us in the pews. No one dared nod off during one of his sermons. (Though I do recall my mother giving my father a poke now and then as his head drooped dangerously close to his chest.) If we wanted to know what was good for the Jews, we learned it from Rabbi Feuer. Communism—bad. Zionism—good. Racism—bad. Civil Rights—good. Quotas—bad. Affirmative Action—good. We heard his take on the day's best sellers, on Supreme Court decisions, on what was new on TV (the emergence of *All in the Family* led to some particularly interesting sermons), and on which issues in the public arena should concern us.

Admittedly, I found him a bit scary. But I knew what my congregation stood for. I knew that I was expected to volunteer to help the vulnerable and that we had to stand up for Soviet Jewry. I knew that I would spend a summer in Israel working on a kibbutz and walk to school on Earth Day. Fortunately, I also had more approachable rabbinic role models among the parade of young assistants who helped translate those messages from "on high" into action.

RABBI MARLA J. FELDMAN (NY85) is currently the interim director of development for the Union for Reform Judaism. Previously she served for seven years as the director of the Commission on Social Action of Reform Judaism.

Perhaps we glorify the past too much, but it seems that the current political tenor of our community makes it more difficult for rabbis to speak out assertively on public policy matters. Of course there are many rabbis who preach passionately about social justice, and I am proud of the leadership role our Movement has taken on issues like Darfur and health care reform. Yet, there seems to be a growing reluctance to take on political issues without shading our messages with so much nuance that we haven't really taken a stand. We bend over backwards to appease those with opposing views lest they feel uncomfortable in our sanctuaries as we endeavor to embrace all people with all views. We temper our message to be as inclusive and nonjudgmental as possible and hesitate to say forthrightly that some views are simply inconsistent with Jewish values. Our hesitance to "afflict the comfortable" is, I fear, to our detriment.

I sense many reasons for this trend over the past several decades: The political environment has become extremely polarized; there is a perception of growing diversity within our community; current political concerns are more subtle and strategic consensus more elusive than in the past; and the role of the rabbi itself is evolving. Examining each of these factors separately may be helpful in understanding where we are today.

The Political Environment Has Become Extremely Polarized

Reflecting only anecdotally, I sensed a shift in how our community responds to political issues going back to the Reagan era. Prior to that, there didn't seem to be a striking difference between Jewish Democrats and Jewish Republicans—most were social liberals, favoring civil rights, reproductive choice, and free speech, but perhaps differing on fiscal matters and labor issues. Since that time, as partisan politics have become more polarized, party adherents also have become more rigid. What was (is) good or bad for the Jews has come to be defined by political parties and their apparatchiks rather than Jewish communal leaders. Liberals and conservatives have been equal offenders, in my opinion.

This split has grown continually over the past several decades, coming to a head during the 2008 election when Jewish Republicans boldly declared that those who cared about Israel should only vote Republican and the countervailing Rabbis for Obama arguing that Jewish values were better reflected in the Democrats' platform. This partisan bickering within the Jewish community has made it virtually impossible for rabbis to speak out on public issues, bearing witness to the moral and ethical teachings of our faith, without being accused of biased political motivation.

As an aside, it is for this reason that I decided NOT to join Rabbis for Obama. Those who know me know my political leanings. However, when I proclaim Jewish teachings to be my rationale for a particular advocacy position, I want to do so without the message being tainted by the perception of partisanship. As individuals, we have every right to engage in partisan political activity in our private lives as long as we keep it out of the congregation. However, as rabbis, I think we can be more effective if we strive to convey that we do not act out of partisan allegiance. Once we are publicly associated with a particular political party or candidate we cannot expect those in the pews to simply disregard that information when they listen to us preach. As they consider the source of any message, I would have them consider my source to be Jewish text and tradition, rather than a political campaign. For me, this means exercising some *tzimtzum* in the arena of campaign activity.

There Is a Perception of Growing Diversity within the Jewish Community

I find the idea of political diversity as somehow a new phenomenon curious, since studies show that the actual voting patterns of American Jews have not changed dramatically in recent years. Yet there is a perception of a recent shift in Jewish voting habits. Perhaps one explanation is that communal leaders today are more likely to be business owners, professionals, and investors than the labor union organizers, teachers, or social workers of a prior generation. Our community's vested interests have changed, even if our values have not.

And clearly, the political minority within our community has found its voice. While certainly this is a good thing, it is a challenge nonetheless. The typical congregant today does not automatically defer to his or her rabbi as the arbiter of morality or the ultimate exponent of Jewish values. Embracing democracy, those in the pews are less willing to sit back and listen to their rabbi challenge their values without demanding equal time or, preferably, a pulpit devoid of anything controversial or personally uncomfortable. There are many within our congregations who would urge us to remain silent in the face of the diversity within our ranks, as political differences threaten the harmonious fabric of congregational life.

Current Political Concerns Are More Subtle and Strategic Consensus More Elusive than in the Past

In addition to the challenges posed by political partisanship, many feel that today's issues are less clear-cut than in the past—or at least less clear than our memories of issues of the past. Afghanistan and Iraq, with their nexus to international terrorism and Middle East politics, are not the same as the Vietnam War was for our community. Advocating for same-sex marriage does not galvanize our community as did freedom riding for voting rights. Opposing parental notification laws is not as dramatic as protecting women from back-alley abortions. It is difficult to be dogmatic about separating church and state when we are not just opposing Christian prayers in public schools but also the ability of a small church in the inner city to receive government funds for its soup kitchen, or financial benefits to our own institutions for enhancing our security infrastructure or for strengthening our day school system. And while Darfur seems to have replaced Soviet Jewry as the cause around which to rally, without any Jewish connection to the issue save our obvious commitment to ending genocide, it is difficult to sustain advocacy or find effective means of engagement.

There are certainly some consensus issues within the Jewish community, yet even on these issues there rarely is uniform agreement as to the appropriate strategic approach to take. For example, does support of Israel mean we want the U.S. government to refrain from interfering in Middle East affairs or do we want our government to play a central role as a peace broker? Does fear of Iranian nuclear aggression suggest we should isolate Iran or engage Iran within the family of nations? Even where there is a general consensus on social justice issues like poverty, health care, or the environment, there are some who would suggest that these are not "Jewish" causes that have a claim on us greater than any other citizen.

The Role of the Rabbi Itself Is Evolving

Compounding these challenges are changes in the rabbinic role itself in relation to our congregants. The rabbinic model that Rabbi Feuer epitomized rarely exists today. The rabbinic role has become more teacher and pastor than public orator. We are as likely to convey Jewish values through Torah study and adult education as through Shabbat sermons or *divrei Torah*. And many of us connect with congregants more deeply through life-cycle ceremonies or congregational programs than during worship services. Many of these changes are for the good. Yet I have a nagging concern that as we come down from "on high" and as "Rabbi Feldman" morphs into "Rabbi Marla," we may find our leadership role diminished in our quest to serve and comfort.

In many communities, the congregational rabbi is no longer seen as the community's primary spokesperson. Congregants do not automatically concede to the rabbi on matters of public concern when many of them have more expertise than we do in public affairs. How do we presume to pontificate about the health insurance crisis, for example, to a sanctuary full of doctors, lawyers, insurance brokers, and business owners? And why would we risk alienating congregants who have strong opposing views in an era when congregations are struggling to maintain membership and fiscal stability?

Finally—I hesitate to actually write these words—a shrinking job market makes it riskier for colleagues to step out on a limb and take potentially controversial stands. For good or for bad, the era of the respected and feared rabbi with a lifetime contract and total freedom of the pulpit is a thing of the past.

Despite all these challenges, speak we must. Whether through a classic three-point sermon, informal *divrei Torah*, bulletin articles, or classes, it is incumbent upon us to apply Jewish values to today's world. As rabbis, it is our job to use all the skills and knowledge at our disposal to keep Judaism relevant and inspire others to live Jewishly. Our leadership role requires us to give voice to ancient truths. However, if we are to be successful in this endeavor, we must also be wise.

Long before a rabbi speaks out on an issue, the members of our congregations should know that Reform Judaism stands for certain principles and that these values will be given voice through our congregations. Though there might be disagreements, there should be no surprises. Even in the best of circumstances, whenever a rabbi or congregation takes a stand on a political issue, there are likely to be some who are unhappy. While that may be inevitable, we can ameliorate the angst of our members by being sensitive and responsive to their concerns and finding ways to make sure they feel that they have been heard. As for our own role as clergy, we need to balance our obligation to lead with the prudence to choose our battles wisely. When we claim to speak in the name of Judaism or Jewish values, we need to first lay the appropriate foundation and engage others in a process that inspires confidence and trust.

Tzedek v. Tzedakah

Given all the challenges and risks, it is no wonder that we often fall back on what is easy and noncontroversial when it comes to our social action mandate. Reform congregations have become experts in coordinating hands-on projects to relieve human suffering: Mitzvah Day programs, interfaith home building projects, public school partnerships, volunteering at soup kitchens and shelters, and providing support services for seniors and other vulnerable populations. We are great at collecting all sorts of items to assist the needy and raising funds for charitable causes. *Tzedakah* and *g'milut chasadim* have been embraced by Reform congregations and this has become a hallmark of our Movement.

This is all to our credit and I would not recommend changing any of this. Through such projects we build community, we raise awareness of human need and societal injustice, and we provide much-needed relief to those who are suffering. And best of all, who could object to such activities? I do not subscribe to the view espoused by a growing number of activists that traditional social action projects are lower than advocacy on some hierarchical scale of justice. If someone is hungry or homeless, railing against injustice and advocating for new welfare laws will not fill their bellies or put a roof over their heads. We must feed and shelter them, first and foremost.

And yet, we know that providing meals for those in shelters and collecting food for soup kitchens is not enough, and it does not fulfill our obligation *lirdof tzedek*—to pursue justice. Relieving the suffering of vulnerable people today is vitally important, but it does nothing to prevent others from experiencing the same plight in the future. We will not effectively reduce poverty without addressing root causes such as the low minimum wage, health care reform, education, or affordable housing. Similarly, cleaning a local park may be important for children in your community, but it will not guarantee that our grandchildren will have clean drinking water or breathable air. Wearing green wrist bands and buying mosquito nets raise critical awareness about the crisis in Sudan and provide some relief to the victims, but putting an end to the atrocities will require advocacy for sanctions and international peacekeepers.

Seeking systemic change at that level requires political advocacy. Hands-on projects alone will not break the socioeconomic cycles that cause suffering and injustice. Changing the nature of our society is subversive—it requires courage and political will. And the changes that need to be made will not be made in soup kitchens; they will be made in the halls of government. And so, our mandate to pursue *tzedek* requires that we embrace the cliché and speak truth to power.

Our congregations will not move to that level of engagement absent a clear articulation of Jewish values backed up by the visionary voice of their rabbi. No matter how great the congregation's social action programming, clergy are not exempt from their prophetic role. A great *tikkun olam* program should not preclude the call for justice also issuing forth from the bimah. Certainly the rabbinic voice will not be the only one raised to these issues, but it is a critical one and its absence will be heard as loudly as its presence.

The Role of Advocacy in Congregations[1]

The rabbinic voice is critical to inspiring meaningful action within the congregation. The most effective social action rabbis are those who mobilize consensus on the vital moral issues of the day and engage the synagogue in a "holistic" congregational social justice program. By "holistic" I mean a combination of hands-on volunteer projects that meet immediate needs, education about both the underlying policy issues and the Jewish foundational values involved, and advocacy to stimulate long-term solutions. This full range of programming will create a meaningful experience for congregants and have a greater impact on society than a more narrow slice of social justice work.

Facilitating the advocacy component of a congregational social justice initiative can be tricky. When guiding a congregation to become engaged in public advocacy, I would propose a three-step protocol:

1. The congregational leadership needs to be nonpartisan, respectful, and open to divergent views.
2. Congregational members need to understand that Judaism, and particularly Reform Judaism, stands for certain things.
3. Congregations need to establish a process for engaging in public policy matters that engenders respect and confidence.

1. The congregational leadership needs to be nonpartisan, respectful, and open to divergent views.

"Political" is not synonymous with "partisan." Being political means being engaged in the world and both rabbis and congregations are permitted—perhaps even commanded—to address public matters. Yet being politically involved does not require partisanship. Of course, the congregation's tax exempt status requires that it remain nonpartisan and not take actions that endorse or oppose a particular candidate or party. Congregational spokespersons should be willing to praise as well as oppose the positions of elected officials of any party when they take actions as our representatives with which we either agree or disagree.

Rabbis are entitled to express their own views from the pulpit, hopefully rooted clearly in Jewish values and interests. Yet we need to be aware that whenever we speak in the public arena we are perceived to be representing the views of our institution, despite any disclaimers we might make. This is both a burden and a privilege and an aspect of our leadership role that requires careful reflection.

When representing our institutions, we should be careful to articulate the consensus positions of those we represent. Remaining sensitive to the fact that most of our members join the congregation for reasons unrelated to its public policy positions, we need to engage them in the deliberative process, educate them about the mission of the congregation, and be prepared to hear opposing views. We can determine whether a consensus exists through public gatherings, educational programs, and by soliciting feedback in our bulletins and electronic communications. And we can work to build a consensus where none yet exists by engaging the congregation in dialogue on an issue through sermons, public forums, studying the Jewish values at stake, and inviting feedback.

2. *Congregational members need to understand that Judaism, and particularly Reform Judaism, stands for certain things.*

When a public policy issue is adopted in the name of the congregation, its leaders should attempt to seek consensus, explore the issue from different perspectives, and engage the membership with due diligence. Nonetheless, they need not be so fearful of dissent that they say nothing at all. "Consensus" is not synonymous with "unanimity," nor is it a guarantee of being right. Diversity of opinion within the pews need not deter the congregation from fulfilling its mission of teaching fundamental Jewish principles, encouraging its members to live rich Jewish lives, and helping to bring Jewish ideals into the public arena. Congregations are not partisan institutions, yet they are driven by a known set of values.

When individuals join a Reform congregation, they know (or should know) that the congregation will act on certain principles. Just as most members know that a hallmark of Reform Judaism is an openness to the "other"—whether lesbian or gay, interfaith families, or those with special needs—they should also know that there will be a strong social action component, including Mitzvah Days, collection drives, volunteer opportunities, education about current issues of concern, and a role for the synagogue to play in communal social justice struggles. They should be prepared for their clergy to speak out on current events, applying Jewish values to issues of the day and challenging the congregation to engage. And it should be expected that the rabbi and the congregation will make a collective effort to bring our progressive, Reform Jewish values to bear in the community at large. They should know that both the congregation and its clergy will be engaged on issues of local, national, and global concern; they will participate in interfaith coalitions and activities; they will use their collective voice to speak out on behalf of the vulnerable and seek justice for all. This is who we are and what we strive to teach our members.

I think Professor Art Green stated this best in an online forum (socialaction.com) several years ago:

> Spreading our most basic moral message—that every person is [created in] the divine image—requires that Jews be concerned with the welfare, including the feeding, housing, and health, of all. The Torah's call that we "pursue justice, only justice" (Deut. 16:20) demands that we work toward closing the terrible gaps, especially in learning and opportunity, that exist within our society and undermine our moral right to the relative wealth and comfort most of us enjoy… In the case of Judaism…a bifurcation of spiritual and sociopolitical concerns is hardly possible. Anyone who tries to undertake it ultimately has to deal with the prophets of ancient Israel, still the strongest and most uncompromising advocates for social justice our world has known. If you try to create a closed world of lovely Jewish piety and build it on foundations of injustice and the degradation of others, Isaiah and Amos will not let you sleep.

It is easier to make this case when we maintain our focus on the Jewish values, ethics, and teachings at stake. That is what brings members to our pews and what they expect to learn within our walls. And therein lies our rabbinic expertise. With a few exceptions, we are not policy experts, and we should not presume to stand in wonky shoes—though we might want to consider inviting such experts to address our congregations and let them speak for themselves. Nonetheless, we are the experts in Jewish teaching and values and our leadership role demands that we bring this knowledge to bear on the work of our congregations. It is in this aspect of congregational social action programming that the rabbi's voice is critical.

3. *Congregations need to establish a process for engaging in public policy matters that engenders respect and confidence.*

When and if a congregation takes on a political issue, knowing that there may be some members who disagree, it needs to be clear that it is the position of the institution, and not necessarily every individual member affiliated with it. Political leaders understand this dynamic; most are themselves members of religious denominations that take positions with which they sometimes disagree.

So, for example, when the Religious Action Center articulates a position taken by the Reform Movement it does so "on behalf of 900 Reform congregations in North America, with a membership of 1.5 million members." While the subtlety of the language could be lost on some, this framing of our size and strength is an honest reflection of who the RAC represents. The RAC does not claim to speak for each Reform Jew, but rather represents the positions of the CCAR and the Union for Reform Judaism, each of which has a clear mandate and process for taking public policy positions.

When an institution like a congregation adopts policy, it should do so with a clear mandate from its constituency and with a process that is known, consistent, and appropriate to its mission. Many Reform congregations take policy positions, yet there is no single process by which they do so. Some have written procedures while others rely on historical precedent. Many congregations defer to their clergy, board, or social action committee to adopt positions in the name of the congregation and a growing number do so through community organizing.

Community organizing has become central to many congregations' social action programs through the Reform Movement's Just Congregations initiative. The techniques used by community organizers to identify key areas of common concern through one-on-one meetings and sharing stories are tools that any congregation can utilize, whether or not they are institutionally aligned with a faith-based community organization. Such strategies are helpful to building a constituency around particular concerns over time so that, once a policy position has been taken by the institution, there are no surprises and general agreement has been ascertained in advance. The success of those churches and synagogues that helped secure passage of the Massachusetts universal health care system stands as a shining example. Was there controversy? Certainly. But two years of one-on-ones and group meetings clarified the consensus that existed and even those who held different opinions had to respect that. Was it political? Yes. But care was taken never to make it partisan.

While there is no uniform procedural model, congregations do not need to start from scratch in adopting policy positions. One place to start is by relying on policies adopted by the URJ, CCAR, WRJ, or MRJ, all of which represent members of Reform affiliates through a democratic process. In addition, the platforms and responsa of the CCAR provide insight that may be helpful in determining whether Jewish values and tradition would provide a foundation for advocacy. The following basic steps might be part of a congregation's process to vet policy positions:

1. Examine the Jewish values that are at stake and consider whether Judaism offers a unique perspective that should be heard. An adult education program, sermon, or school curriculum can provide the unifying spark that leads to congregational action.
2. When committees or boards are empowered to take positions in the name of the congregation, it is with the understanding that there will be a fair and balanced process. Be sure the decision-making body is comprised of a diverse membership, with multiple points of view represented and heard. Congregants should have opportunity for input.
3. Consider having a procedure for time-sensitive matters that would allow the leadership of the congregation to act more quickly. Such a process might include agreement among the rabbi, president, and social action chair, in consultation with others, or convening the executive committee with a conference call.
4. Triage! With so many issues facing us, congregations need to be selective and carefully consider on which issues to take a position. These are some of the factors that congregations might consider in winnowing down the list of issues to address:
   - Are there Jewish values at stake? Does the Reform Movement have policy on this issue?
   - Is this issue particularly timely? Is there a piece of legislation, a ballot initiative, or other governmental action about to take place that requires immediate input?
   - Is this an issue where the Jewish voice is particularly noteworthy? Do we, as Jews, have something unique to add to the public debate? Are there interfaith coalitions in search of a Jewish partner?
   - Is this an issue that resonates for a significant number of congregants? Is this an issue around which we can generate interest and activity? Do our members care about this issue?

- Will this issue have a significant impact on the lives of our congregants? On our community? On our society?
- Is this issue an extension of other activities and priorities to which the congregation already is committed? Will taking a position on this issue support a larger initiative or otherwise amplify an existing project?

5. Act on the policy, once adopted. Once a position has been taken, it is essential that the membership of the congregation be informed and engaged. Background and educational information should be provided to clarify the rationale behind the policy taken along with action suggestions.

There are many steps along the road to advocacy—education, dialogue, action—and we should not short-change any of them on the route to the finish line. Sometimes a stirring sermon will be the beginning of a process, sometimes the end, and sometimes it will not be about the sermon. But rabbinic engagement and leadership will always be critical to the pursuit of justice. We may not have the carte blanche that prior generations of rabbis had to rail against injustice from the safety of the bimah, but if our message has integrity and we have laid the proper foundation, we will have born our prophetic mantle well.

To be is to stand for...

— Abraham Joshua Heschel

Note

1. I first presented much of the following material in the Union for Reform Judaism manual *Speak Truth to Power: A Guide for Congregations Taking Public Policy Positions*, which is available online at www.urj.org.

Ritual Versus Justice: Must We Choose?

Suzanne Singer

As a rabbi, I have been engaged in a debate for many years with my colleagues about whether one's involvement in both ritual observance and social justice is a zero sum game. In other words, is it the case that the more time one spends on observance, the less time is available for social justice, and vice versa? In a recent exchange with me in *Sh'ma*,[1] Rabbi Richard Levy, one of my most significant mentors, explained that, as president of the CCAR, one of his reasons for spearheading the new Reform Principles of 1999 was, "to correct the perception—if not the reality—that increased ritual observance, prayer, and study were crowding out the movement's historic commitment to social justice."[2] My response was that, all too often, this is in fact the reality. A case in point: When I was a student at Hebrew Union College in Los Angeles just a few years ago, *t'filah* was increased from twice to four times a week. Where students once made lunch for the hungry some mornings before school, now they prayed, a change pointed out by my esteemed colleague, Rabbi Linda Bertenthal, in her excellent senior sermon.

Not that we should have to make choices between the two. As Rabbi Levy points out, "Both—sanctifying time and place, and working for peace and justice among the peoples God created—were part of our mandate to 'bring Torah into the world.'"[3] And indeed, ritual and justice are intricately interconnected. To quote Rabbi Levy again, "Social justice needs to include study and worship (in the streets before a protest, for example), and worship to be effective needs to involve liturgical study...we must ask how

---

RABBI SUZANNE SINGER (LA03) is rabbi/educator at Temple Beth El in Riverside, California. During her rabbinate, she has been actively engaged in social justice work, having organized two social justice conferences, in 2005 and 2007.

our prayers can spill out of Shabbat use to affect the ways we relate to God at home, in nature, and in the public square."[4]

Indeed, it is actually quite difficult to make a distinction between the ritual and the ethical mitzvot. When I first taught about mitzvot during an Introduction to Judaism class, I tried to separate them but quickly discovered that it was almost impossible to do so. For example, if we take the commandment to observe Shabbat, it soon becomes clear that this mitzvah encompasses myriad ethical concerns. To begin with, we are told in the Torah that we are to give our servants, as well as our animals, a day of rest, certainly one of the very first expressions of concerns for worker and animal rights in history. Then, our willingness and ability to slow down, to connect to our deepest values, to spend time with those dearest to us, underline what matters most in life. This realization should lead us to treat our fellow human being with respect; it should prevent us from exploiting others, particularly in pursuit of money and power. Finally, the mindfulness we develop through Shabbat observance should instill in us a sense of gratitude for the blessings we have, sharpening our awareness of what so many in the world are not so fortunate to have.

The real issue is: Does observance, in fact, lead to this kind of mindset? And if it does, are we prepared to "pray with our feet," as Abraham Joshua Heschel described his marching for civil rights? Edward Feinstein, senior rabbi of Valley Beth Shalom in Encino, California, asks what the most important word in the prayer book is. His response: *"al-ken*—therefore."

> "Therefore" connects all our fine sentiments and deep wisdom with the reality of the world. "Therefore" binds us to bring our values out of the vague realm of our subjectivity and into the hard objective world of work, family, politics and power. "Therefore" tests all our spiritual aspirations and visions against the limits of our courage, imagination and resolve. "Therefore" makes religion real. Every day, someone confesses, "Rabbi, I'm a deeply spiritual person."
>
> Good, I reply. Where's the "therefore"? What difference does it make? How does your spirituality shape the way you spend your money, speak to your housekeeper, raise your children? Do you vote spiritually? Drive spiritually? Watch TV spiritually? I am little impressed by those who profess to believe in God. I am moved by those whose faith is behaved. That's my "therefore" test.[5]

Kashrut is another example of how ethical concerns are intertwined with ritual observance. The Torah's rationale for observing kashrut is so that we can be holy. In addition, kosher slaughter has been considered the most humane way of killing an animal. Certainly, holiness and concern for the animal should also encompass our concern for the slaughterhouse worker. Thus we should expect that the kashrut *hechsher* stand for decent wages and working conditions, not only proper *shechitah*.

Unfortunately, observance does not guarantee morality, and all too often observance for observance's sake becomes the norm. I am not sure how many observant Jews combine dietary practice with awareness of kosher slaughterhouse conditions. Just look at the recent scandal surrounding Agriprocessors, the largest glatt kosher meat packing plant in the country. Not only were the animals treated appallingly, but the workers, many of whom were undocumented so with little recourse, were also paid very low wages under dangerous and unhealthy working conditions . According to a 1996 article in *The Forward*, for example, workers claimed that they received "virtually no safety training. This is an anomaly in an industry in which the tools are designed to cut and grind through flesh and bones. In just one month…two young men required amputations."[6] It is gratifying to know that the Conservative and Reform movements are developing an additional kind of *hechsher* called Magen Tzedek, though I wish this would be an unnecessary move: the traditional hechsher itself should be a guarantee of righteous conduct.

I fear that with greater observance has come greater insularity, however. I remember a conversation with some of my fellow students in seminary who stated that they liked to go to kosher markets and restaurants in order to run into others who keep kosher. My response was that I liked going to non-kosher markets and restaurants to run into everyone else. For several decades now, because the Jewish community has been so concerned about the problem of continuity, Jews seem to have retrenched from their concern with the larger society and reached inward to fortify their Jewish identity. This has been particularly true for some of my colleagues. They believe that this focus on social justice is the old Reform Judaism that jettisoned all the traditional rituals. They want synagogues to move us back to tradition; they want our congregations to spend more time in prayer and study, and to increase observance of mitzvot. Indeed, in the past decade, the Union for Reform Judaism (URJ) has launched initiatives to increase Jewish literacy through an emphasis on Torah study, and in the past year, at the URJ's Biennial, Rabbi Eric Yoffie challenged synagogues to reinvigorate Shabbat morning services. Certainly these are worthy goals. But the question is: To what end? What is the answer to Rabbi Feinstein's "therefore"? Are we becoming more observant for the sake of being more observant, to fortify ourselves as Jews for the sake of our Jewish identity? Or is there an additional reason for the preservation of our rituals?

Social activist Leonard Fein, founder of *Moment* magazine and MAZON, expresses this beautifully:

> ...the central American Jewish problem of our time is not anti-Semitism, nor is it intermarriage specifically or assimilation more generally. It is the problem of boredom, the fact that for very many American Jews, the experience of being Jewish does not seem to be about anything—not, at any rate, about anything that matters very much. Many Jews are simply unable to fill in the blank in the sentence that begins with the words "It is important that the Jews survive in order to...." In order to what? In order to survive?
>
> I can think of no single statement to which more Jews through the centuries and even today would subscribe, no sentence that more accurately and comprehensively captures the most fundamental Jewish insight, than that this, our world, God's world, is not working the way it was meant to—and that to be a Jew is to know that, somehow, you are implicated in its repair.
>
> Accordingly, the completed sentence reads, "It is important that the Jews survive in order to help repair this oh-so-fractured world."
>
> ...in the end, it is not the services we attend that will sustain us; it is the services we perform. For us, Shabbat was never meant as a stopping place; it was meant as a resting place, a place to regather our energies to take up again, and forever, God's work in this world.
>
> And what is that work? Do we not know? Have we not been told? It is the work of clothing the naked and feeding the hungry, of embracing the stranger and freeing the captive and smashing

the idols; it is, in short, the work of justice. That is the Torah that we are instructed to do. That is the Torah that drives us.[7]

In our recent *Sh'ma* exchange, Rabbi Levy asks: "What does the greeting 'Shabbat Shalom,' imply? Are we as a movement ready to join the conversation on how and when to disengage from Iraq? Are we ready to encourage young people to carry the URJ resolution on the war to sources of influence in this country? Are we ready to raise our voices to counter those in the Jewish community who are content with the status quo in the Middle East?"[8] I too hope that our prayers for shalom are not idle chatter. Indeed, how can we pronounce such words in synagogue if we are not willing to actively promote peace? Here, we are not talking about making a choice between prayer and social justice. Rather, we are asking that the ethical implications of our ritual mitzvot be uppermost in our minds—and on the doorposts of our house. I have frequently been "accused" of being a classical Reform Jew. Though I am not one, I do miss the universal outlook of classical Reform, the focus on the prophets' demand for justice. I am not looking to return to its stripped-down version of Judaism, but I would like to see more of us embrace the causes championed by our impressive Religious Action Center. I would like a concern for others and for *tikkun olam* to infuse our observance, our prayer, and our study. And I would like to see us leave the pews and take to the streets or the legislature or the op-ed pages of our newspapers.

In today's high-stress society, the truth is that, all too often, people don't have time for both observance and action. Choices must be made: spending Saturday morning at services or at a homeless shelter? Engaging in *t'filah* or making peanut butter sandwiches for the hungry? And while we shouldn't be considered inauthentic Reform Jews if we are equally concerned about separating milk and meat as we are about the working conditions in factories, what about the reverse? If our focus is on the latter, does that make us any less authentic? Were our classical forefathers less Jewish because they eschewed kashrut and *kippot*? And do we admonish Jews who never go to shul but are engaged in fighting for living wages? If some of us don't have the time to be at the forefront of social change, shouldn't we honor those who do? When the Israelites marched through the desert, the tribe of Dan brought up the rear, gathering those who had fallen behind. The Torah commentary *Etz*

Hayim explains that Dan was chosen because the Danites loved their fellow Israelites even though their religious faith was weak. "There is a need in today's community for people who express their religious faith by caring for the left-behind."[9]

According to recent studies, though young Jews want to be involved in social service, they are not so attached to Judaism. They fail to see the connection. They often view Judaism as irrelevant, boring, and obsolete. If the Reform Movement is to have relevance for our youth, we must make it crystal clear how Jewish tradition can respond to the urgent concerns of the day. An example: Recently, fast food giant Burger King joined major restaurant chains in establishing animal welfare standards in its choice of suppliers. I wish our Movement had been at the forefront of pushing for this reform. We could have made the connection between the humane treatment of animals and kashrut. Let us offer our youth a revitalized tradition that moves us beyond the borders of our own community and into the public square. Let us infuse our ritual, prayer, and study with the urgent call to right the wrongs of society. And let the Reform Movement again make a priority of speaking truth to power.

Notes

1. Richard N. Levy and Suzanne Singer, "(Re)Defining Reform(ing)," *Sh'ma* 38, no. 645 (November 2007/Kislev 5768): 8–10, www.shma.com.
2. Ibid., 8.
3. Ibid.
4. Ibid.
5. Edward Feinstein, "Are You Listening?" *JewishJournal.com* (August 3, 2006), http://www.jewishjournal.com/torah_portion/article/are_you_listening_20060804.
6. Nathaniel Popper, "In Iowa Meat Plant, Kosher 'Jungle' Breeds Fear, Injury, Short Pay," *The Jewish Daily Forward*, May 26, 2006, http://www.forward.com/articles/1006/.
7. Leonard Fein, "And Pursuing Justice" (keynote address delivered at the 64th UAHC Biennial Convention, Religious Action Center of Reform Judaism, October 31, 1997).
8. Levy and Singer, "(Re)Defining Reform(ing)," 9.
9. David L. Lieber, ed., *Etz Hayim: Torah and Commentary* (New York: Rabbinical Assembly, 2001), 825.

Dissent from the Dissenters

Clifford E. Librach

I

The Reform Movement owes its birth and life to dissent. From the earliest days of its European conceptualization through its regnant and triumphal contemporary domination,[1] the Reform Movement in Judaism[2] has sought validation as a legitimate historic alternative to any of several more traditional extant models of Judaism. Its leaders and spokesmen have used the depth and vastness of the Rabbinic tradition, traversing across thousands of years and thousands of miles, to establish that this movement is not a radical rejection of so-called Rabbinic tradition as much as it was and is a rejuvenation and restoration of the same.[3]

Evidence of alternative textual readings and accepted exceptions, of acknowledged conundrums and validated normative corrections all have been found, cited, and massaged to bolster the historic legitimacy of Reform as a valid and grounded alternative articulation of modern Rabbinic Judaism. In its continuing and fundamental dissent from traditional models of Judaism, Reform has cloaked itself in the mantle of a vast and tolerant tradition that famously is expressed in the Rabbinic aphorism *"Eilu v'ellu,"* "These [words] and these [words] are both [though they articulate diametrically opposed opinions] the words of the living God."[4] They are both valid, they are both right, they are both accepted, they both must be seen as legitimate and determinative not only for each aboriginal scholar and his respective followers,[5] but for subsequent communities and—ultimately—movements. This despite the fact that they are (in many cases) in direct normative conflict and often cannot, in any real sense, coexist.[6]

Differences—for example, in the style of lighting Friday night candles by which to welcome Shabbat—are legion. Every pulpit

---

CLIFFORD E. LIBRACH (C86) is the rabbi at the United Jewish Center, Danbury, Connecticut. He received his J.D. from New York University School of Law in 1977.

rabbi knows that there are as many varieties of candle lighting styles as there are Jewish homes—and that nearly all of them are "valid" inasmuch as such venerated home-based ritual traditions are often validated by memory and mimicry more than by punctilious attention to detailed instructions.

But this is not all of Judaism. There is much—indeed very much—that is not simply reduced to a matter of taste and style, of (perhaps sloppy or faulty) memory and mimicry. And so Reform has dutifully, for example, taught "how to" light the Chanukah menorah or "how to" recite the Four Questions in Hebrew or "how to" recite *Kaddish* in Aramaic—fully acknowledging that these are standard ritual objectives the correct performance of which is valued.

Yet against these (and other) basic ritual rubrics there remains a vast network of Jewish "correctness" to which Reform respectfully dissents, not merely as to "how to" or "how not to" perform this or that detail, but whether the entire category belongs in Judaism's appropriate modern articulation. Here the fundamental standards of kashrut come first to mind. But to this must be added a dissenting posture regarding nearly the entirety of regulated Jewish life: the nature and restrictive character of Shabbat and *Yom Tov* observance, for example; the form, composition, and complex technical web of the various rubrics of prayer and worship embedded in the liturgy; and the claim of the vast network of God-inspired Jewish obligations (mitzvot) and its concomitant system of Rabbinic regulation—known by the tradition as halachah—as the canvas upon and within which achievement, creativity, justice, and righteousness are to be found and mastered each day by each Jew. As to all of this, Reform has stood in the posture of dissent.[7]

And as dissenters, Reform has sought and even demanded validation, not through normative embrace as much as through tolerance and acknowledged historic plausibility. Reform leaders and spokesmen have routinely sought refuge for their alternative vision in the protection of Rabbinic and Jewish history. This or that alternative, it is often said, is a plausible rendering—is yet another possible variation among the many that have illustrated the vast Jewish landscape of the past. Ours is at least as reasonable a reading of the often contentious past as is that deemed somehow more proper, if clearly not more popular. And therein has lain the brightest shining badge of Reform's honor, now abundantly evident for all to see: it is popular.

Indeed, as a phenomenon of sociology—as opposed to ideology—the Reform Movement in Judaism may best be appreciated and understood. It has articulated a rendition of Judaism, with its emphasis on individual human autonomy and choice (however much that is circumscribed by the inherited Rabbinic tradition) that has dovetailed perfectly with the modern American ethos. Individual human freedom—unmediated by rabbinic authority or halachic strictures—has fit with sustained facility the secular American way of life, with its deep cultural emphasis on individuals over family and tradition and its commitment to overthrowing the old inherited way in exchange for new and unprecedented opportunities for individual achievement.

But the sociology of the Reform Movement in Judaism must be measured alongside the sociology and social psychology of all American Jews. For them—Jews predominantly descendant from Eastern European Jewish stock arriving on these American shores in the late nineteenth and early twentieth centuries—the seemingly narrow religious definition and God-centered self-image upon which all Jewish religious movements stand has proved inadequate. The counter-identity is spoken of as "cultural Judaism" and is known by its total rejection of Judaism qua religion as a basis for behavior or values. Much more than religion, cultural Judaism has embraced ethnic history as its lodestar of value formation and behavioral justification.

Also inherent in the ideological glue of cultural Judaism in America has been an embrace of twentieth century liberal politics.[0] The reasons for this unmistakable tilt to the left are the subject of some debate and contention, but the validity and predictability of the leftward tilt is beyond cavil. For many, liberal politics is the religion of the American Jews. And this preoccupation has saturated the Reform Movement as well.

The manifestations of this general condition are everywhere and always. They are in the political hue and character of the plenum resolutions adopted each year by the CCAR and the URJ. They are in the shock and discomfort expressed by rabbinic search committees, congregational governing boards, or random gatherings of self-identified Reform Jews, that a rabbi would not articulate the prevailing "orthodox" (meaning here: standard, determinative, and enforced) political position on this or that public issue. Even beyond the shock and discomfort is the deprecation of the integrity and very decency of any who might raise a deviant nuance in its face. The range of issues is vast, each one with complex threads running through the entire American political landscape: be it abortion rights and its public funding; tax and welfare policy; war and peace, most especially and most recently the Second War in Iraq; public assistance in any manner—including that authorized by law—to those (including Jews) who are sending their children to religiously endorsed and authorized schools; the impregnability with which a "wall of separation between church and state" should be seen to undermine the (Constitutionally protected) free exercise of religion by American citizens; the persistent demand that a "scientific consensus" (against which all skepticism is a troglodyte blasphemy) requires a wholesale reshaping of the world's resource allocation and economy and the immediate repair of its immoral imbalance now in favor of American resource consumption and material prosperity; or the expansion, through the lens of "bioethics," of the use of legal mechanisms, voluntarily by individuals and their next of kin, to terminate human life. There are other issues.[9] These are but examples. But make no mistake: the political climate of the American Reform community is orthodox.

Against this orthodoxy I have been a dissenter. And I have found the Reform landscape, ironically itself born of ideological dissent, to have been breathtakingly intolerant.[10]

Always (I hope) cognizant of my capacity to err in logic and reason, always willing to engage, learn, and correct and not withdraw, retreat, and sulk, I have sought through my career to observe the charge of the great prophet Micah[11] with an open mind, distinguishing between ends and means. Slogans, bumper stickers, and clichés have all frustrated and repulsed the scholar in me, which insists that nuance and subtlety are finer hallmarks by which to be known than is predictable orthodox obedience. I acknowledge as well the siren song of being in opposition for its own sake, the lure of an "over against" psychology that has its own seeds of self-righteous corruption. In the face of these dangers, I remain utterly convinced of the vast irony that I and some few others have faced. If "liberal" means open, tolerant, accepting, curious, nonjudgmental, and accessible to new thoughts, ideas, and resolution, then contemporary liberals and leftists are not. This may be among the great ironies of our or any time in modern political thought: liberalism has ceased to be liberal.[12]

II

Is dissent valued in Judaism? This is a fundamental question for a system that obviously values multiple readings of its inherited texts while simultaneously asserting the authority to determine and enforce individual ritual and ethical behavior and conduct.

The classic device of Rabbinic midrashim is instructive. These literary excursions, often filling in the interstitial gaps of the Torah text, offer a vast array of alternative biblical readings (alternative, that is, for the purpose of creative and didactic exposition). Their centrality to the Rabbinic enterprise demonstrates an embedded tolerance for reinterpretation in light of time, place, culture, and perspective. The question is often not whether this or that reading is right, but rather what forces—coming from without and emerging from within—animated the re-visioning. Midrashim on the same verse can coexist and simultaneously be contradictory. A tradition that values such contradictions has welcomed varied interpretive glosses as competing legal or moral lessons. The effect is achieved by the manipulation of words inherited without vowels and sometimes with peculiar spellings. It has revealed the biblical text, in dramatic contradistinction to fundamentalist Christianity, as an ever-malleable clay in the potter's hand, whose "meaning" is the continuing subject of creative enterprise, not the dry presentation of historic and authoritative resolution.

And yet, this tradition of creative readings is not without limit or boundary. Some explanations are efforts to resolve context and clear meaning,[13] while others are plainly fanciful or even playful or clearly artistic excursions to demonstrate the virtue of an ethical value or a political objective. But it is the continuing technique of interpretation—not rejection, excision, or the haughty representations of moral superiority in the face of decrepit primitive values—that gives life to the midrashic process. Rabbis interpret their way through the biblical text, not by cutting and pasting, or selectively celebrating or rejecting, but by massaging the meaning of words and the hierarchy of values they project. As if to say in the face of each verse or fragment, "You *could*, of course, look at it *this* way instead," the midrashic tradition leaves an extraordinary legacy of dynamic insight, creativity, and wisdom.[14]

In addition to the tradition of rabbinic midrash, there are two simple facts implanted in the inherited Jewish tradition—one scriptural and the other Rabbinic—that testify to an embrace of dissent and of self-criticism that together set this tradition apart as nothing less than a celebration of disputation.

There is no ancient tradition that has so preserved and even glorified its own brutal and unmitigated self-criticism as has Judaism, in the corpus of the *N'vi-im*, the words of the prophets of Israel. These readings are replete with bitter denunciations of moral lapses and excesses, historic failures, and cultural shame directed by our prophets against ourselves. Though we are often challenged to discern just what it is that the prophets are saying, the *tendenz* of their remonstrations is clear: the Jews are a people with God-inspired potential but also with the capacity for gross moral turpitude, repugnant popular values, insidious corruption, and self-deception.[15]

And why are the words of the prophets of Israel preserved and repeated, heard again and again and again, if not to animate and justify the eristic impulse? We are endowed with angel-like capacity, to be sure, but are ever-burdened by our own blindness and dark side. We need to turn the magnifying scope to the inside, on ourselves, and dissent from what is common, what is habit, what is customary, conventional, unquestioned, and assumed—from what is routine. The prophetic tradition teaches, inter alia, the virtue and necessity of dissent from what is popular and accepted, from the mainstream of ourselves.

But even beyond this scriptural hallmark, the tradition of dissent is most clearly celebrated by the plain fact that from the very beginning of the Rabbinic enterprise, minority opinions were preserved. Why?

They—minority opinions—are essentially of no legal significance,[16] but from the earliest era of the Mishnah and the artistic disputations of the *zugot*,[17] they have been dutifully recorded and preserved. Why? We are speaking here of a tradition—a legal tradition—that predates Anglo-American jurisprudence by some seventeen hundred years. That is also a tradition known by the hallmark of the preservation of minority opinion, but opinions to which reference can later be made and even adopted in a theoretical process of self-correction.

Not so Rabbinic Judaism. Though much effort is made, for example, to understand and even justify and anticipate the messianic correctness of the oft-minority opinions attributed to the sage Shammai and the school that bears his name[18] there is no immediate legal value in the preserved opinions that are not binding, valid, or applicable. They are clearly and obviously preserved for the sake of their intellectual and philosophical integrity, for the sake of their logic and probity, for the sake of their critical value in testing the justification of the majority. Minority opinions are not to be discarded. Rather, they must be confronted; they must be answered; they must be given attention, weight, and value. Even though normatively inapplicable, they are invaluable to intellectual discipline and comprehensiveness.

III

Beyond these simple and structural truths that demonstrate the value of dissent, there is in the lore of Rabbinic decision-making, complete with its central axiomatic tradition of majority rule, a tale that by clear inference celebrates not only disputation, but nonconformity. The tale is justly famous. But it is told almost always as a tender celebration of a benign and charmed Deity, chuckling as His or Her human servants grapple with the legal here-and-now, and in so doing toy with apostasy. It is usually commended as a paean to the independence of human reasoning.[19] The story moves beyond its charming but penultimate conclusion, however, into a dark and haunting tragedy of Rabbinic intolerance and narrow-mindedness.[20] It is this tail of the tale that is seldom recounted, explored, or confronted.

The Rabbis, assembled as at a conference table, have been arguing back-and-forth about the ritual purity of a certain oven belonging to a man named Aknai.[21] Is the oven, in a word, kosher or not?

Rabbi Eliezer is taking a minority position and has brought forward every conceivable argument in support of his legal position that the oven is indeed kosher. The other rabbis are united in their opposition. And so the story continues:

> Then he [Rabbi Eliezer][22] said to them [the other rabbis]: "Even the carob tree can prove that the law is as I have argued!"

> And the carob tree uprooted itself and moved one hundred cubits away. Some even insist that it moved four hundred cubits away.

But the other rabbis said to him: "A carob tree cannot serve as proof."

So he [Rabbi Eliezer] then said: "If the law is as I have argued, then let the stream of water right here prove it!"

[And] the stream of water began to flow backwards.

But they [the other rabbis] said to him: "A stream of water cannot serve as proof."

Again, he [Rabbi Eliezer] said to them: "If the law is as I have argued, then let the walls in the House of Study prove it!"

[And] the walls in the House of Study began to incline.

But Rabbi Y'hoshua rebuked them and said to them: "if the scholars argue with each other about the halachah, what business is it of yours?!"

The walls did not, therefore, fall down completely—out of respect for Rabbi Y'hoshua. But out of respect for Rabbi Eliezer, they also did not straighten up completely again. They yet remain standing in an inclined position.

He [Rabbi Eliezer] then said to them: "If the law is as I have argued, then let Heaven prove it!"

And, in fact, a [Heavenly] Voice proclaimed: "What do you want from Rabbi Eliezer? Don't you know that in all matters of law the decision is in accordance with his opinion!"

At that, Rabbi Y'hoshua jumped to his feet and shouted: *"Lo bashamayim hi!"* "(It is not in Heaven!)"[23]

What did he mean by [that quotation from Deuteronomy] *Lo bashamayim hi*?

Rabbi Jeremiah explained: "Since the Torah has already been revealed at Mount Sinai, we give no heed to a further [Heavenly] Voice. After all, at Mount Sinai You have written in the Torah itself the principle that, in legal matters, 'the vote of the majority is decisive!'"[24]

> Later, when Rabbi Natan met Elijah, he asked the prophet: "What did the Holy One, praised be He, do at that hour?"
>
> Elijah replied: "He chuckled and said: 'My children have defeated Me! My children have defeated Me!'"

That is usually the end of the telling.[25] The story seems complete and closed—a lesson in the independent power, virtue, and integrity of human endeavor as against even divine fiat. God has no vote in the human Rabbinic court, which is endowed by God's own authority (i.e., the Torah) to resolve legal questions of correct behavior and ritual convention. The majority has spoken and even God can be and will be overruled by the prevailing number.

But there is not where the story ends. It continues. Rabbi Eliezer was severely and harshly disciplined for the protestation of his lonely minority voice.

> On that very day [of the dispute regarding the oven of Aknai] every single object that Rabbi Eliezer had declared to be kosher was brought forward and burnt by fire [as now not kosher]. Then they [the assembled rabbis] took a vote, and excommunicated him.
>
> They [looked at each other and] asked: "Who is going to go and tell him [the news about his excommunication]?"
>
> "I'll go," said Rabbi Akiva, "lest some irresponsible person go and tell him and in so doing destroy the whole world [by being crude and brusque]."
>
> So what did Akiva do? He put on black clothes and wrapped himself all in black [like a mourner] and sat down four cubits from [Rabbi Eliezer].
>
> "Akiva," said Rabbi Eliezer, "what's the news of today?"
>
> "My teacher," he replied, "it seems to me that [your] colleagues are standing apart from you [having put the *cherem*-ban upon you, which means none of us can ever be physically close to you again]."
>
> At that point he [Rabbi Eliezer] too tore his clothes [like a mourner], pulled off his shoes, pushed back his stool, and sat on the floor while tears poured from his eyes.

The whole world was at that moment struck: one-third of the olive crop, one-third of the wheat crop, and one-third of the barley crop were destroyed. Some even say that the dough in the hands of women [became sour and] expanded [at that moment]. A *Tanna* taught: Great indeed was the calamity of that day, for everything upon which Rabbi Eliezer focused was burnt to a crisp. Rabban Gamliel [who was the Nasi, or President of the Sanhedrin, and was Rabbi Eliezer's brother-in-law] was traveling by ship, when a gigantic wave rose up as if to drown him. "It seems to me," he muttered, "that this is on account of nothing other than Rabbi Eliezer ben Hyrcanus."

At that moment, he stood up and prayed: "King of the Universe! You know full well that I did nothing [in this matter] for myself, nor for the honor of my family name, but rather for Your honor—so that disputation would not multiply in Israel!" At that moment, the roaring sea subsided.

Ima Shalom was Rabbi Eliezer's wife—and was the sister of Rabban Gamliel. From the time of the incident [of the dramatic vote concerning the oven of Aknai and the subsequent imposition of the *cherem*-ban], she did not permit him [her husband] to recite *Tachanun* [the daily penitential prayers by which Jews confess their sins]. [She was afraid that if her husband would pour out his bitter grief to God, that the Almighty would compensate by holding the head of the Sanhedrin—her brother—Rabban Gamliel responsible and mete out divine punishment.] Well, a certain day…[she became confused and thought it was a day on which he did not have to recite *Tachanun*, so she relaxed her watch over him]. She returned from her distraction and found him in the posture of penitence [as is customary for the recitation of *Tachanun*]. "Get up!" she screamed to him, "You've killed my brother!"

At that very moment the sound of a horn came from the home of Rabban Gamliel—that he had died.

"How did you know this?" [Rabbi Eliezer] asked her.

"I have a tradition from my grandfather's home: All gates may be locked; but never the gates of isolation and humiliation."[26]

Now told to its proper and compelling dénouement, it is a tragic story—not of divine charm at human pretense to authority, as is usually its suggested moral. No, this vignette concludes with tragic consequences for Eliezer, for his wife, for her brother, and for the Rabbinic Academy. It is a story of intemperance and abuse of power, of intellectual intolerance and the undisciplined disrespect and rejection of dissent. And its kerygma is just this: woe to those who squelch or discipline the articulation of nonconformity.

The Reform Movement in Judaism was born of a protestant ethic, a quest for normative correction that required challenge, disagreement, and rejection of the enforceable status quo. Its legacy is not simply tarnished but surrendered when it embraces ideological rigidity and a correlative intolerance of dissent, disputation, and challenge. Righteousness needs no majority, and ideas—religious and political—are cheapened when imposed and undefended. The integrity and rigor of the enterprise are at issue and at stake. Dissent is the blood of Judaism.

Notes

1. The most recent exposition of the triumph of the Reform Movement in America, and its attendant deficiencies in leadership and responsibility, can be found in the excellent analysis by Jack Wertheimer, "What Does Reform Judaism Stand For?" *Commentary* 125, no. 6 (June 2008): 31–37.
2. I advisedly use this formulation, rather than the often proffered "Reform Judaism" by way of insistence that it remains possible to see Judaism as a vast and complex river, with often wide and eroding banks, but nevertheless with boundary and border intact. Whether this image can be long sustained in the face of increasing radical Reform departures from normative Jewish standards of identity and alarming trends of assimilation in America is not the subject here, but beckons serious attention. In his superb review of the intellectual foundations of Reform, this formulation was used and justified by intellectual historian Michael Meyer. See Michael A. Meyer, *Response to Modernity: A History of The Reform Movement in Judaism* (New York: Oxford University Press, 1988).
3. Regarding its early European phase, this point is comprehensively demonstrated in Jakob J. Petuchowski, *Prayer Book Reform in Europe: The Liturgy of European Liberal and Reform Judaism* (New York: The World Union for Progressive Judaism, 1968).
4. BT *Eiruvin* 13b.
5. See note 18, *infra*.
6. This axiom introduces, of course, a fascinating thread in a legal system committed, by definition, to the avoidance of anarchy. Rabbinic Judaism thus does not permit *eilu v'eilu* to trump, as it were,

the fundamental principle of *achar rabbim l'hatot* (majority rule), Exod. 23:2; BT *Sanhedrin* 29a, or to suggest that any articulated opinion on any subject is ipso facto of equal and binding legal applicability. It stands alongside other generalized standards that amplify a dynamic and tolerant tradition of law and interpretation, but that should not be read as vitiating the very function and life of normative regulation. See note 14, *infra*. *Sh'vi-im panin l'Torah*. (The Torah has seventy faces.) *B'midbar Rabbah* 13:15, for example, is understood as tolerating an abundance of levels of interpretive gloss, but not accepting all renditions as equal and valid. In *Pirkei Avot* 5:20 it is famously observed that any *machlochet* (controversy) *l'sheim shamayim* (for the sake of heaven) is sure, in the end, to lead to final resolution (*sofah l'hitkayem*). The key phrase is the final one (*sofah l'hitkayem*). Those who value *a final resolution* and not simply a disputation for its own sake, are presumptively a part of a sustaining community grounded in a legal network of regulated behavior. See note 7, *infra*. All of this applies whether one is speaking of the four corners of a real legal system, with applicable and enforceable norms of behavior, or of *hashkafa*, a theoretical world of justification or personal philosophy. *Hashkafa* is, after all, merely the halachah of the mind.

7. Of course there have been many attempts over the years, including my own, to articulate some measure of "Reform halachah" or to fashion a theory or hermeneutic by which Reform could find a place along the interpretive spectrum of Jewish law. The intellectual nobility of these efforts notwithstanding, the absence of an antecedent self-identifying community committed to Jewish normative regulation has made and makes such projects little more than hyper-intellectual sport. The Conservative Movement, now adrift in a miasma of confused and undetermined halachic/non-halachic self-imagery, is in danger of stumbling into the same linguistic trap. We may speak the language of "ought" and "should" and "should not" but if there is no validating antecedent community—no "buy in" as modern culture would have it—then the exercise is little more than a high-brow, asymptotic game of justification in a parallel universe.

8. This phenomenon is the subject of an insightful volume by Norman Podhoretz, which broadly speculates but leaves finally unresolved the reasons for this fascinating and sustaining generalization. Norman Podhoretz, *Why Are Jews Liberal?* (New York: Doubleday, 2009).

9. It is worth noting that the vectors seem to widen a bit when the issue concerns the security of the State of Israel. But I am not at all sanguine about this prospect. In 2009, officers of the CCAR, without consultation, debate, or referendum gratuitously criticized Israel's policy vis a vis settlements in the West Bank, insisting that

they were an impediment to "peace." And ample anecdotal evidence is in circulation amongst rabbis, to-wit: that rabbinic search committees are asking more and more about Israel with an eye toward objection to its government as a sincere seeker of peace with her neighbors.

10. Anecdotes abound, but it is not the purpose or thrust of this effort to catalogue evidence or regale readers with a feast of woeful tales. Let one such story be representative: a rabbinic search committee at a prominent Midwestern congregation had found in me (after a three-day in-person review) a positive and attractive candidate for their open pulpit. But "rumors" had circulated that my "position" on abortion was not the acceptable mantra. A hastily arranged conference call was scheduled, and a prominent attorney on the search committee was assigned to interrogate the candidate. "Are you pro-choice or pro-life?" demanded my interlocutor. "I am both," was my admittedly cunning reply. I continued, "Judaism cannot be reduced to a slogan or a bumper-sticker or a phrase. It is filled with nuance and subtlety and indulgence in the complication of details." My interrogator stammered with annoying frustration (as the job prospect rapidly flowed down the drain), "I don't care about what Judaism says! I want to know what YOU think!!" *Quod erat demonstrandum.*

11. Mic. 6:8. "It has been asked: What does *Adonai* require of thee? Only to do justly, love mercy, and walk humbly with your God."

12. This deeply ironic achievement that liberalism itself tends toward its ideational opposite—like a cone on its side with its ever-narrowing vectors of tolerance facing the future—is one of the signal observations of the modern political zeitgeist by the great literary and social critic Lionel Trilling. Lionel Trilling, *The Liberal Imagination: Essays on Literature and Society* (New York: Doubleday, 1950). Note well that anti-Semitism, once the preferred bigotry of the right wing, is now masked as the campaign to delegitimize the State of Israel, and has moved across the political spectrum in the last fifty years to now be coexistent with left-wing causes, movements, and culture. And the reign of so-called political correctness, restraining so much open expression in American academia in the name of human sensitivity—thus attempting to prohibit all "offensive" speech—is a project of the left.

13. So to resolve the *p'shat*, or the plain, contextual, grammatical reading of a text, as opposed (in the Rabbinic idiom) to the *remez* (the hinted meaning), the *d'rash* (the implicit meaning), and the *sod* (the esoteric or secret meaning). BT *Chagigah* 14b.

14. But note well that this creative and dynamic technique has its obvious limits and is to be distinguished from the distinct and parallel world of traditional biblical commentary. Every biblical text has its context. One verse, one passage, one narrative tale must be

analyzed against the vast inherited corpus, not read as if it stands alone without position or relevance to its textual surroundings. And so it is that though there is a creative interpretive enterprise (apart from the midrashic project) at work when interpreting the words of Scripture, some explanations are indeed better—more preferred—than others. Those interpretations that offer a greater coherence—and less literary fragmentation and anarchy—as regards the biblical totality, are better, more complete, more competent, more worthy, than those with less. All interpretations are accordingly not equally "valid." Some are better than others and indeed one—elusive as the messianic promise itself—is the best. The notion of one best or most comprehensive and most coherent interpretation that incorporates the largest context is explored and defended famously in jurisprudence by Ronald Dworkin in *A Matter of Principle* (Cambridge: Harvard University Press, 1985) 119-177; and *Taking Rights Seriously* (Cambridge: Harvard University Press, 1977): 81-130. The same principle: namely that one best explanation or interpretation is, however elusive, a point of quest or a sustaining desideratum, can apply to biblical exegesis as well.

15. I do find it almost charming to note that there was a period of classical Reform Judaism when Reform rabbis proclaimed that theirs was a reincarnation of "Prophetic Judaism"—a Judaism denominated by a tradition of social and political self-criticism. Apart from the obvious and rather cheap practice of cherry picking the prophetic verses that seemed to excoriate all ritual at the expense of moral rectitude, this elevation of "the prophets" was indeed never constructively ritualized. First of all, the prophets of Israel railed against hypocrisy—not ritual per se, but insincere ritual. And the prophetic tradition of Judaism is ritualized in the reading of the weekly haftarah, often reduced or even discarded by Reform praxis. Note, for example, that the haftarah reading for Shabbat Morning was eliminated at the UAHC Biennial convention in Atlanta in 1997, "in order to save time."

16. As in any legal system, there are some extremely rare exceptions to this rule. But the standard is reliably stipulated: a *posek*—a rabbinic decisor of Jewish law—cannot base his ruling upon a minority opinion in the Talmud. There are, of course, myriad cases of *machmir* (stringent) and *meikil* (lenient) rulings on similar or even identical questions. But these are always justified by the applicable massaging of the facts and inherited legal literature—Mishnah, Talmud, Codes, and relevant *t'shuvot*. Minority opinions are essentially of no legal significance.

17. Pairs—dual sets of scholars conjoined as classic interlocutors in *Pirkei Avot* 1:4–15. Each pair was contemporaneous, one the *nasi* (president) and the other the *av beit din* (chief justice) of the Sanhedrin. The period of application was just prior to the Maccabeean

Revolt in 167 B.C.E. to the period before the *Tannaim*. The five *zugot* were Yosei ben Yoeizer/Yose ben Yochanan; Y'hoshua ben Perachiya/Nattai of Arbel; Y'hudah ben Tabbai/Shimon ben Shetach; Shemaya/Avtalyon; and the most famous: Hillel/Shammai.

18. Beit Shammai; the effort to understand their rulings, contrary to the accepted rulings of the eponymous Hillel and the school, Beit Hillel, which follows him, is found at BT *Y'vamot* 31a–b.
19. No one less than my teacher at New York University School of Law, the much heralded Professor of Jurisprudence and Legal Philosophy Ronald Dworkin, expressed fascination and wonder at the "genius" embedded in this story, which he found compelling as a brilliant statement on the nature of law itself and the role of judges/decisors in deciphering, articulating, and justifying it. R. Dworkin, *Jews and Justice: Ronald Dworkin on Jewish Law and Interpretation* (December 7, 2005) (CD).
20. In this analysis, I am indebted to my revered and honored late teacher, Dr. Eugene Mihaly, *zt"l*, who first suggested to me this modern tradition of incomplete popularization. We spoke of it often. His insight and sensitivity were crucial to my understanding that dissenters, though plainly surrounded by a dissenting milieu, are often lonely and abused.
21. The famous story of the oven of Aknai is told at BT *Bava M'tzia* 59b. All translations are mine.
22. This is the same Rabbi Eliezer ben Hyrcanus who is one of the five "sages of B'nei Brak" included in the famous legend told in the Passover Haggadah, along with Rabbi Y'hoshua ben Chananya, Eliezer's *baal t'risin* (shielded adversary) in this story. A third sage of B'nei Brak was Rabbi Elazar ben Azariah, appointed at age eighteen to succeed the imperious Gamliel, President of the Sanherdrin and brother-in-law of Eliezer, who bore personal and ultimate responsibility for the harsh manner by which Eliezer will be subsequently and finally disciplined.
23. Deut. 30:12.
24. Exod. 23:2, as interpreted by the Rabbinic tradition.
25. See, for example, Jakob J.Petuchowski, *Our Masters Taught: Rabbinic Stories and Sayings* (New York: Crossroad, 1982), 43–44; Francine Klagsbrun, *Voices of Wisdom: Jewish Ideals and Ethics for Everyday Living* (New York: Pantheon Books, 1980), 349–50.
26. Rabbi Elazar ben Azariah (the successor to Rabban Gamliel as the Nasi of the Sanhedrin) is quoted as saying "Even though the gates of prayer have been locked since the day of the Temple's destruction, the gates of tears have never been locked." And in the name of Rabbi Shimon bar Yochai, the Gemara teaches that "it would be better for a man to throw himself in a burning furnace than to seek to humiliate his fellow in public." BT *Bava M'tzia* 59a.

When Rabbis Take Positions
Principles of Rabbinic Advocacy

Same-Gender Marriages from the Intersection of Faith and Politics

Arthur Gross Schaefer and Robert Cornwall[1]

Last year's passage of Proposition 8 in California, outlawing same-sex marriages, represents a combination of political and religious agendas that rabbis need to publicly address, so that faith-based considerations, from a Jewish perspective, play a greater role in framing the continuing debate over this issue. While one can parse the motives and thinking behind the 52 percent[2] of California voters who adopted Proposition 8 last November, it is important to view the controversy over same-sex unions along the historic intersecting lines between faith and politics from a Jewish-Christian standpoint. In light of the increasing acceptance of same-sex marriages,[3] understanding and incorporating religious perceptions are critical as various groups supporting same-gender marriage discuss whether to attempt a reversal of Proposition 8 in 2010 or 2012. However, it is stunningly clear that this support "has come entirely from the ranks of registered Democrats and nonpartisans rather than Republicans."[4] With the latest polls suggesting that support for same-sex marriages among California voters has stalled at less than 50 percent,[5] an understanding of both the religious impact and the role of rabbis to help structure the tone of the discussion

---

RABBI ARTHUR GROSS-SCHAEFER, J.D. (NY84) serves the Community Shul of Montecito and Santa Barbara and chair of the Department of Marketing and Business Law at Loyola Marymount University, Los Angeles, California.

REV. DR. BOB CORNWALL is the senior minister of Central Woodward Christian Church (Disciples of Christ) of Troy, Michigan and editor of *Sharing the Practice: Journal of the Academy of Parish Clergy.*

could well mean the difference between passage and defeat in the next round of propositions. Those colleagues and their communities who frame the issue of same-sex marriage solely as a civil rights issue and argue that religion is an inappropriate interloper, ignore the reality that religion has been and will always be a part of our national dialogue on major political topics.

The authors of this paper are a Christian pastor and a rabbi who have worked together for years and are of the opinion that faith has a public dimension—that faith is not a private entity that should be kept out of the public realm and that the language of religion should be made a component of the dialogue by moderate rabbis as a way to attract religious-based individuals to more progressive positions on particular subjects, while at the same time, rustle away the label of sole religious legitimacy from the Religious Right. On one hand, there is the complex topic of how elected officials and political parties should respond to faith communities that wish to be heard on matters of public concern. There are both constitutional and spiritual issues involved in this inquiry concerning how religious persons are to become involved in political life themselves. It is not only the political parties that face difficult questions, but the various religious traditions as well—mainly those whose theologies and practices differ from one group to the next.

Of the two major political parties, the Republican Party seems to be the most comfortable with religious input, and many candidates go out of their way to court religious voters. Indeed, the so-called Religious Right has considerable institutional linkages to the party, so much so that many observers on the left have warned about theocratic tendencies within the Republican Party. For religious persons who are politically progressive, the Democratic Party may be a more natural fit; there is, however, discomfort both within the party structures and among politically active people of faith as to the most appropriate way of engaging each other.

Many candidates and leaders within the Republican Party have, in recent years, framed political issues in moral and religious terms. On the other hand, Democrats, for a variety of reasons, have shied away from making a strong connection between religion and politics. This has led to the charge that Democrats are unfriendly to religious voices. While Democratic Party leaders have, on occasion, spoken openly of their faith and how it has influenced their political lives,[6] there is clearly a general discomfort with public statements of faith, along with a belief that such actions are contrived political tactics. At the same time, politically progressive religious persons have begun to articulate positions seemingly harmonious with the Democratic platform, even though they are not always identical.

Ways of Approaching the Conversation of Same-Sex Marriages in a Religious Context

The relationship between institutional religion and the political realm has been a matter of debate from the beginnings of the nation's history. Although Christianity—especially Protestantism—has dominated America's public life, history has shown an aversion to making the correlation official. There has always been a strong civil religion element present, usually taking on broader tones as opposed to denominationally specific ones, and any attempt to declare America a Christian nation has been rebuffed.[7] "In God we Trust" and similar confessions of faith appear on currency and stamps. The Ten Commandments and biblical verses adorn the walls of courthouses, schools, public buildings, and even the Liberty Bell. Crucifixes and other Christian symbols were erected in state parks and on state house grounds for a significant part of our history.[8] Christmas and Easter are official public holidays. Sunday remains an official day of rest and many states still have blue laws limiting activities on this Christian holy day. Government sponsored chaplains are found in Congress, the military, prisons, hospitals, and other government settings. The President of the United States is sworn in using the words "so help me God" and lights a Christmas tree on the White House lawn. Clearly, an endorsement of religion, or at least certain religious concepts, exists at some level. It would appear that this is an endorsement of a civil religion, representing religious concepts that were commonplace in the early unfolding of the American experiment.[9] Rather than reflecting religious dogma, these concepts were seen as cultural norms that were fundamentally adopted by most citizens. To put it another way, these doctrines were core values that supported and nurtured a newly forming democracy. We hold on to these values for their historical significance and as a reference point, a touchstone to help guide us in the turbulent waters of the present and future. Still, the bond between religion and public life, official or not, has been close.

Historian Mark Toulouse[10] has developed a helpful taxonomy for understanding this relationship. While Toulouse's focus is on Christian involvement in the public square, it can nevertheless be helpful to rabbis considering their own involvement. He outlines four approaches to engagement, which reflect the majority of America's Christians yet also have important insights for other religious traditions including Judaism: iconic faith, priestly faith, the public Christian, and the public church. Iconic and priestly faith, he posits, are expressions of a civil religion, with the remaining two options attempting to separate spiritual and earthly matters where the church speaks not as part of the establishment but as a prophetic challenge to the establishment.[11] Toulouse argues that the latter two models should be used for religious involvement, while rejecting the first two, claiming that civil religious concepts confuse and bind religious and public ideologies together with symbols. He believes iconic and priestly faith styles undermine the integrity of the state and various religious entities as the United States struggles with being Christian, Judeo-Christian, or none of the above, and other religious traditions fight to make their voices heard.[12] A brief review of these four models applied to liberal rabbis may provide important insights when engaging public discussion regarding same-gender marriages.

Iconic Faith

The flap over Keith Ellison's decision to take his oath of office using the Koran illustrates the nature of iconic faith, which is often associated with civil religion. With iconic faith, a religious symbol, such as the Bible, may take on nationalistic meaning. In this case, the Bible is seen as a totem that serves to guarantee one's trustworthiness. Or, a public symbol such as the flag is venerated as a holy object, and so burning the flag is seen as desecrating a sacred image. In both situations, the majority faith is merged with national interests, establishing the belief that God is seen as being predisposed to favoring the nation. An iconic faith requires a homogeneous setting, and thus, religious pluralism is discouraged (at best). The religious community in this form of engagement is largely passive, since the activism emanates from the side of the state. For rabbis involved in the gay marriage conversation, civil religious concepts are tied to those areas where there is already a common agreement that furthers the civil and civic nature of the nation state. Clearly, issues surrounding gay and lesbian rights were neither foundational concepts nor do they have general acceptance in the public sphere, the necessary components for inclusion within iconic faith. Even the principles of an individual's right to privacy used for *Roe v. Wade* or the human rights ideals in the civil rights amendments, all of which have become part of our civil religion, would be considered ineffective to those who limit civil religion to fundamental concepts that were present and accepted in the early development of the nation. Simply put, this is a doctrine that should not be used in the current discussion on same-gender relationships.

Priestly Faith

The belief that America is a Christian nation reflects the concept of priestly faith. The nation is seen as the vehicle for God's work in the world. In America, with one supporting the other, the nation and Christian faith are intermingled. The nation looks to the church for moral support, while the church in turn looks to the state for financial and legal support. National interests take on the aura of divine missions and national agendas are wrapped in God-language. Priestly faith tends to be legalistic, and religious norms (Christian in this case) define what is acceptable behavior for citizens. With regard to the priestly faith, the religious community takes on an activist position and sees itself as the protector of cultural values. Thus, the American vision is God's vision—indeed, this is the foundation of Manifest Destiny. Again, in such a view of public engagement, pluralism is suspect if not discouraged, and faith can become exceedingly coercive. For example, the colony of Connecticut adopted the Puritan religious tradition, establishing laws against heresy and banishing dissenters.[13] The Puritans felt called by God to establish a "new Israel," a Holy Commonwealth based on a covenant between God and themselves as the people of God. In the hope of establishing a new Jerusalem, The Puritan colonies of Connecticut and Massachusetts were to be examples to the world of God's kingdom on earth, "a City upon a hill."[14]

Those who were not of a colony's chosen religion were often angry at the requirement to pay taxes supporting the state religion. For example, the Baptists of Connecticut deeply resented a legislature that presumed to pass laws regulating churches and taxing citizens purely to support the Puritans.[15] Puritan leaders left little room for individual religious experimentation as dissidents were summarily dismissed and immigration specifically restricted Jews, Catholics, and Muslims.[16] Generally, most rabbis see the evident problem with this doctrine as the majority religion—which does not include Judaism—claims dominance and adherence. As a minority religion within the United States, rejection of such a doctrine is critical to our own survival and obviously not helpful for rabbis in the debate on same-gender relationships.

If iconic and priestly faiths are inherently problematic, both from a governmental and from a religious perspective, faith can engage with the public square in other ways. Toulouse speaks of these as the public Christian and the public church perspectives. Although Toulouse directs his particular study at the Christian community, the ideals are transferable, in our minds, to any religious tradition including Judaism, though again, this does not appear to be a useful model in a public discussion of same-gender relationships.

Public Person of Faith

St. Augustine and Martin Luther both conceived the religious and the political realms as being radically separate. Luther called these two realms the two kingdoms of God and the world. In one sense these perspectives recognize a "wall of separation" between church and state.[17] As the "public person of faith," one can enter the public square and allow one's faith to influence how to engage public life, while the religious community remains focused on spiritual matters. Therefore, the community can nurture a prophetic spirit for its adherents, but as an institution, it will remain outside the public debates. From this perspective, involvement spans from nonparticipation to individual activism, but the congregation does not enter the business of transforming the nation or the world. Furthermore, there is a range of attitudes towards pluralism from a concern over radical forms to an embrace of more moderate pluralism.

Judaism, which is clearly focused on community in terms of prayer and celebration, along with a definite halachic focus on the many responsibilities that one has to the community, would therefore have major difficulties with this attempt at a definitive separation. Our prophetic tradition is for Jewish communities to see their spiritual beliefs conducted through direct social action as a way to fulfill the mandate to help repair the world, *tikkun olam*.

Public Religious Community

The final option of public religious community seems very promising for rabbis who wish to support same-gender marriages. Such a means of engagement makes necessary the recognition that God's reign covers both secular and sacred realms. From this perspective God is concerned about the world itself and calls the community of faith to advocacy for justice. Public activism is rooted in both faith and the communities themselves, not just religious individuals, as they begin the process of transforming the world. Martin Luther King Jr., who called on not just individuals of faith, but also communities of faith to overturn racism in America and enact civil rights legislation, may best illustrate such an approach. The community becomes prophetic and active. The more individualistic expression of public engagement tends to see sin in personal ways, whereas this form acknowledges the systemic nature of sin. Thus, the community of faith works toward not just the redemption of the individual, but the social redemption of the world. Political activity is an essential component of one's faith and part of the community's mission. The danger is the narrow line separating such a view from a priestly faith. At what point does the faith community that seeks justice cross the line into coercion? The path away from priestly faith requires humility and a retreat from absolutism.

Such an approach is also well grounded in our American experience. It is not true that a separation of church and state has led to the death of religion or even the exclusion of religion during public debates. Actually, God and religious concepts are present within our government and used as important considerations when deliberating issues of public concern. Clearly, the matter of abortion and considerations surrounding gays and lesbians involve powerful religious overtones. The Civil Rights movement had, as its base, a deep religious vision. It would appear that religion has had and continues to generate a deep impact on the nation and its policies. It has even been stated that the United States is arguably the most religious of all the industrialized nations, where religious beliefs are not only at the center for millions of Americans, but have shaped the policies and social views of this country.[18] The assertion that a separation of church and state may actually promote the use of religious values and consideration in the national arena may seem like an oxymoron. However, when one critically looks at what has happened in the United States, it becomes obvious that there is an important logic to the strong presence of religious traditions in our public discussions and activities. When rabbis articulate this principle, they are building on a well-developed foundation in our history as well as clearly mirroring our biblical prophetic tradition.

When rabbis point out, as Rabbi Harold Schulweis did many years ago, that homosexuals were made to feel as though they were not human, normal, or even created in God's image, the rabbinic voice reflects those of our ancient prophets who call for just treatment.[19] Many rabbis assert that Jewish law is not without a heart or soul and therefore must be understood to provide for respect and fair treatment for those on the margins of society including the gay and lesbian. Moreover, the biblical view of rebellious children recorded in Deuteronomy 21:1, the case of the *sotah*, the wife suspected of adultery without evidence (Num. 5:12), and laws regarding the sale of one's daughter into slavery or the treatment of false prophets have all been relegated to another time. They therefore should not be enforced today, just as the laws dealing with homosexuals should not be used as a guide for Jewish practice. When rabbis speak clearly that Jewish tradition is not frozen in time but responds to new scientific information and current psychological understanding, we appreciate the biblical phrase that one should live by the laws rather than die by them (Lev. 18:5) as a demand to view religious traditions as guidance but not governance. Rabbinic voices representing an ancient tradition can give validity to a modern appreciation of the plight and yearning of gay men and women not only to be treated fairly but to be treated equally under the law.

A Way Forward

There are inherent dangers in mixing religion and politics, and rabbis must be careful of their involvement with partisan efforts.

There are legal and tax ramifications that must be kept in mind and many believe it is not appropriate for clergy to become heavily involved in partisan issues not supported by all members of a particular clergy's community.[20] On the other hand, how can a religious leader keep quiet if there are important values at stake? Therefore, if clergy and people of faith feel they need to set foot into the political realm, certain matters need to be considered. Besides legal issues, there are also ethical ones. As clergy with sympathies for the Democratic Party enter conversation with the party of their choice, it is important that neither party nor person of faith feel beholden to the other. Clergy must not take on the role of kingmaker or inappropriately use their influence to dictate policy. They can, however, offer words of advice and guidance from the perspective of faith. There can be no quid pro quo relationships where clergy expect some form of benefit when they endorse or support a particular candidate. Indeed, the question standing before both political and religious communities as they begin discussion is whether one or two issues have the ability to trump all others.

If, as we believe, there is room for fruitful conversation and collaboration between people of faith and political parties (in our case, the Democratic Party), we have formulated two sets of questions, one set for religious leaders and the other for politicians.

Three Practical Questions for Rabbinic Leaders

- **When I take a position as a person of faith with political implications, how is faith related to this decision?** Is this position authentically rooted in the Jewish tradition, so that my faith urges me to take this position? Or, have I taken a political position and sought support for it in my religious tradition?
- **As a rabbi, what considerations are involved if I choose to give my pulpit to a politician or candidate who supports same-gender marriages?** In other words, by allowing this person to speak am I making either an explicit or an implicit endorsement of this person?
- **In what ways is it permissible for a rabbi to endorse a candidate? And is taking a position on an issue the same as endorsing a candidate?** Regarding the latter, taking a position on a politically sensitive issue, when must I seek permission of my board or other governing body?

Three Practical Questions for Political Leaders and Organizations

- **Can I use my personal religious doctrines in making political decisions?** Should politicians be able to refer to their personal faith when taking a vote or a position? Or, should politicians be asked to separate personal beliefs from a duty to represent their constituency or even, like a judge in a trial, be expected to separate personal views when acting as a representative of the people and follow the general values of pluralism enshrined in the Constitution?
- **Can I use faith doctrines publicly when pushing a particular policy?** When making an argument in the public square, can I use actual quotes and doctrines from faith traditions to support my position? Or should I resist framing political issues in religious terms?
- **If one strongly believes in the separation of church and state, how do you deal with religious leaders and faith communities that want to become involved in a particular issue or campaign?** Perhaps you are concerned or even dismayed as you see religious groups and faith leaders attempt to control political agendas and suggest litmus tests for candidates? Perhaps you are even very distrustful toward offers of support from religious organizations. And yet, there are religious leaders who want to get involved. How should this relationship between religious groups and political organizations be appropriately developed and fostered?

How one answers these questions may depend on one's theological/faith positions, the polity of one's tradition, and matters of law. For many rabbis, it is not the legal barriers that are the most imposing; instead it is the diversity of political views in their community that constrain one's voice. For many political activists, the answers may depend on their experiences with religion and religious leaders, as well as current political realities. Nevertheless, religion has always been part of our landscape and these issues must be raised, but realistic answers must also be sought that can lead to healthier relationships between religion and politics. In dealing with the future, answers may in some degree require all to ask: Are we willing to become prophetic?

It is our prayer that this article will provide some guidance and consideration for colleagues to develop their rabbinate with both integrity and effectiveness.

A special thank you to Kathe Segall, administrative assistant, and Matt Kagawa, undergraduate research assistant to Dr. Gross-Schaefer.

Notes

1. This began as a position paper written for the California Democratic Party Faith and Values Community Summit held in Goleta, California, on June 3, 2007. Committee members who helped critique and steer this paper included the two authors, the Rev. Jarmo Tarkki, Jon Williams, and Alexis Donkin. Later, an article was developed for a primarily Christian audience and was published as "Faith and Politics: Finding a Way to Have a Fruitful Conversation," *Congregations*, Summer 2008. This article is based on and borrows heavily from these earlier works and ideas expressed by the committee members listed above.
2. *Los Angeles Times*, August 12, 2009.
3. Many gay rights groups have favored returning the issue to voters as soon as 2010. Leaders at Equality California, which spearheaded the campaign against Proposition 8, have said they want to make sure they can win. Ibid.
4. Cynthia Laird, "California Support for Same-Sex Marriage Still below 50 Percent, Says New Report," *Bay Area Reporter*, August 6, 2009.
5. Ibid.
6. The three top-tier Democratic candidates in the 2008 presidential primary season, Hillary Rodham Clinton, Barack Obama, and John Edwards participated in the Sojourner's conversation in May 2007, broadcast by CNN.
7. See Jon Meacham, *American Gospel: God, the Founding Fathers, and the Making of a Nation* (New York: Random House, 2006).
8. John Witte, "The Essential Rights and Liberties of Religion in the American Constitutional Experiment," *Notre Dame Law Review* 71, no. 3 (1976): 406.
9. Ibid.
10. Mark Toulouse, *God in Public: Four Ways American Christianity and Public Life Relate* (Louisville: WJK Press, 2006).
11. B. Cornwall, Book Review of *God in Public: Four Ways American Christianity and Public Life Relate*, Ponderings on a Faith

Journey, March 11, 2007, http://pastorbobcornwall.blogspot.com/2007/03/god-in-public-four-ways-american.html.
12. Ibid.
13. Charles Haynes, *Religion in American History* (Alexandria, VA: Association for Supervision and Curriculum Development, 1990), 49.
14. Charles Haynes, *Finding Common Ground: A First Amendment Guide to Religion and Public Education* (Nashville, TN: The Freedom Forum First Amendment Center at Vanderbilt University, 1994), 3.6.
15. Haynes, *Religion in American History*, 49.
16. Witte, "The Essential Rights and Liberties," 379.
17. The Wall of Separation of Church and State is often credited to Thomas Jefferson. There are several scholars who would suggest that Roger Williams was the first one to suggest this concept as enshrined in his famous *Bloody Tenants*.
18. Haynes, *Finding Common Ground*, 3.2.
19. Rabbi H. Schulweis, a sermon entitled "A Second Look at Homosexuality," delivered December 1996, http://vbs.org/rabbi/hshulw/homo.htm.
20. David Gushee, "Some Rules for Christians in Politics," http://www.faithinpubliclife.org/content/news/2007/07/some_rules_for_christians_in_p.html. Gushee offers seventeen rules, which are extremely restrictive on the role clergy and churches should play.

The Ballot, the Bimah, and the Tax Code

Ellen P. Aprill

There are those involved in synagogue life who insist that synagogues risk loss of exemption and the ability to receive tax-deductible contributions if their leaders engage in political discourse of any kind. Others believe that so long as clergy do not explicitly endorse or oppose any candidate for public office, they are free to engage in political commentary of any kind. Neither is true.

Charities, including churches and synagogues, fail to satisfy the requirements for exemption from income tax under section 501(c)(3) of the Internal Revenue Code if they "participate in, or intervene in (including the publishing or distributing of statements) any political campaign on behalf of (or in opposition to) any candidate for public office." For purposes of this article, I will describe this prohibition as the "political campaign intervention." In contrast, the tax code permits synagogues, like other charities, to lobby—to attempt to influence legislation—so long as such lobbying activities do not amount to a "substantial part" of their activities. Furthermore, charities, including synagogues, may take positions on public policy issues without limit. In brief: no political campaign intervention, some lobbying, and unlimited policy discussion.

While these distinctions are relatively clear in broad outline, the Internal Revenue Service (IRS) enforces the political campaign intervention prohibition against both explicit and indirect endorsement or opposition. The prohibition of indirect political campaign intervention blurs the edges of all three of these categories. The

---

ELLEN P. APRILL is the John E. Anderson Professor of Tax Law at Loyola Law School in Los Angeles. She is a former president of Temple Israel of Hollywood and has spoken and written frequently on issues of pulpit expression and the tax code.

lack of guidance as to what is "substantial" for purposes of the lobbying limitation further complicates the landscape.

Charities, moreover, can speak on these matters in various ways—through resolutions, newsletters, programs, and, in the case of synagogues, from the bimah. For the purposes of the tax laws, rabbis often act in an official capacity, and in that role, their actions can have consequences for the tax status of their congregations. At other times and in other ways, the tax laws recognize that rabbis speak as individuals, with the full protection of First Amendment rights. Distinguishing when rabbinic speech is deemed that of the individual and when it is attributed to the synagogue is crucial. That is, rabbis need to know when their voice and actions have consequences for their congregations as institutions subject to the federal tax laws rather than for themselves as individuals.

This article explains briefly how the IRS distinguishes these categories. To do so, it includes examples, background, and current developments. A full discussion of all the issues and questions that arise in this area of the law will not be possible, however, and thus a list of helpful references is included at the end of the article. The goal of the piece is to help rabbis understand this area of the law so that they may navigate within its strictures, such as they are.

Background and Purpose of the Political Campaign Intervention Prohibition

Lyndon B. Johnson introduced the political campaign intervention ban as an amendment to section 501(c)(3) during a Senate floor debate on the 1954 Internal Revenue Code. No legislative history contemporary with the legislative change explains the purpose of this prohibition. Legislative history from 1987 explains that the ban "reflects a Congressional policy that the U.S. Treasury should be neutral in political affairs."[1] The fact that a number of other categories of tax-exempt organization are permitted to engage in political campaign intervention undercuts this rationale. These other categories of tax-exempt organizations, however, are not eligible to receive tax-deductible contributions. Thus, a more persuasive justification for the prohibition is that Congress did not wish to allow tax-deductible contributions to be used for political campaign intervention.

Constitutionality of the Political Campaign Intervention Prohibition

The First Amendment states that "Congress shall make no law respecting an establishment of religion or prohibiting the free exercise thereof." Thus, many have argued, an absolute prohibition on political campaign intervention for religious groups is unconstitutional. It is incumbent for many, if not most, religions to speak out on political issues, the argument continues, and the need to speak truth to power may require intervening in political campaigns to address the key social issues of the day to carry out that religious obligation.

The courts, to date, have not been sympathetic to this point of view. The most recent is a 2000 case, *Branch Ministries v. Rossotti*.[2] Four days before the presidential election in 1992, the Church at Pierce Creek (the Church) ran full-page advertisements in *USA Today* and the *Washington Times* urging Christians not to vote for then-Governor Clinton because his position on such issues as abortion and homosexuality violated biblical precepts. The ads also solicited tax-deductible contributions. The Court of Appeals found that the Church failed to demonstrate that revocation of tax exemption for political campaign intervention substantially burdened its free exercise rights. According to the court, "the Church does not maintain that a withdrawal from electoral politics would violate its beliefs. The sole effect of the loss of tax exemption will be to decrease the amount of money available to the Church for its religious practices. The Supreme Court has declared, however, that such a burden 'is not constitutionally significant.'" The court affirmed the revocation of the Church's exemption.

Not all believe that this decision has resolved the constitutional issue. The Alliance Defense Fund (ADF) has sponsored two annual Pulpit Freedom Sundays in late September.[3] Ministers participating in Pulpit Freedom Sunday preach about how Scripture applies to every area of life, including, if they choose, candidates for election. As the ADF explains on its Web site, it has organized Pulpit Freedom Sunday in hopes that the IRS will revoke the exemption of at least some participating churches so that the ADF can challenge the constitutionality of the political campaign intervention prohibition. The ADF reports that eighty-three churches participated in Pulpit Freedom Sunday in 2009, as compared to thirty-two churches in

2008, although it is not clear how many ministers engaged in political campaign intervention by endorsing or opposing candidates for public office. The ability of the IRS to investigate the churches that have participated in Pulpit Freedom Sunday has been hampered, however, by a recent court decision that the procedures the IRS has been using to authorize examinations of churches does not satisfy the applicable statute, which has special and particular requirements for any church audit. The IRS has recently proposed new regulations to cure these procedural infirmities and is expected to resume investigations once the regulations become final.

Whether or not the Constitution requires that churches be allowed to intervene in political campaigns, a number of legislators and scholars have called, and continue to call, for some loosening of the prohibition as a matter of policy and prudence. Some proposals, for example, would permit churches to engage in political campaign intervention in communications to members or during regularly scheduled services. One such provision, the Houses of Worship Political Speech Protection Act, proposed and defeated in 2002, would have paralleled the current provision for lobbying activities by providing that churches would qualify for exemption so long as no substantial part of their activities consist of participating or intervening in a political campaign. The Religious Action Center (RAC) strongly welcomed its defeat. Rabbi David Saperstein, in a press release from the RAC, described it as a bill that would have "jeopardized the integrity of religion and the political process," embroiling "houses of worship in divisive battles as to which candidates to support or oppose, undercut campaign finance laws, and led to extensive government monitoring of church political activities."

Legislative proposals to modify the political campaign intervention prohibition surface regularly and the ADF remains committed to mounting a constitutional challenge to it. Thus, this is an area that calls for continued vigilance and monitoring for those involved in synagogue life.

Political Campaign Intervention—
Express Endorsement or Opposition

When questions about political campaign intervention relate to express candidate endorsement or opposition, the parameters of the prohibition are for the most part easily understood. As a result of the statutory prohibition, congregations cannot make contributions to any candidate's campaign, display a banner endorsing or opposing a candidate for public office on their building or on their Web site, or send a letter to their members urging them to vote for or against a candidate for public office. All of these would constitute direct intervention in a political campaign.

The political campaign intervention prohibition applies only to the campaigns of individuals for public office. The IRS has interpreted these requirements in various kinds of public guidance.[4] The public office can be at any level—federal, state, or local. It includes elected judges, school boards, or dog catchers, if they are elected by the public. (Action in support of a judicial nominee who must be confirmed by a legislative body, such as a Supreme Court Justice, is considered lobbying, not intervention in a campaign for public office, and is subject to the lobbying limit, discussed below.) The election need not be contested or involve the participation of political parties. "Candidates" for public office are generally those who have offered themselves or been proposed by others for elective office. Speculation about a prominent person's future run for office does not make the person a candidate. An individual who has formally announced an intention to seek election is considered a candidate. If actions are taken by an individual or by others to further the goal of candidacy, an individual could be considered a candidate even before a formal announcement.

As the challenge mounted by the ADF indicates, however, the political campaign intervention prohibition extends to clergy acting in their official capacity. Thus, a rabbi cannot endorse a candidate from the pulpit, in the congregational newsletter, or at a congregational event, however precious the principle of freedom of the pulpit. Both in a document that has a degree of precedential authority and in a publication designed specifically to guide churches,[5] the IRS takes the position that even disclaimers by the clergy that their remarks represent their personal views do not cleanse such remarks made in official organization publications or at official functions.

In one example in the IRS publication *Tax Guide for Churches and Religious Organizations* ("Church Guide"), not only did a minister's column state that it was his personal opinion that a particular candidate should be reelected, but the minister also took care to pay from his personal funds for the portion of the cost of the newsletter attributable to his column. Such efforts were to no avail. Because the endorsement appeared in the official publication of the church, the example concluded that it constituted political campaign intervention attributed to the church. Similarly, because a rabbi speaks in her official capacity from the bimah or at a synagogue function, an endorsement or criticism of a candidate for public office from the bimah or at any synagogue event would be attributable to the synagogue. Emphasizing that the remarks were the rabbi's own personal opinion and that members of the congregation should decide themselves how to vote would not change the result.

At the same time, rabbis do not lose their First Amendment rights and remain free to endorse candidates when acting in their individual capacities. The Church Guide offers two examples. In one, a minister endorses a candidate at a press conference three weeks before an election, an endorsement reported in an article on the front page of the local newspaper in which the minister's position and church are identified. In the other example, a candidate publishes a full-page ad in the local newspaper listing five prominent ministers who have personally endorsed the candidate. The ad indicates the position and affiliation of each minister. The ad states, "Titles and affiliations of each individual are provided for identification purposes only." The candidate's campaign committee pays for the advertisement. In both examples, the IRS concludes that because the minister did not make an endorsement at an official church function, in an official church publication, or use church funds or other assets, the actions did not constitute prohibited political campaign intervention. The Church Guide also urges religious leaders who speak or write in their individual capacity to indicate that their comments are personal and not intended to represent the views of the organization.

For the most part, congregations easily avoid express endorsements. A report on an IRS Political Activity Compliance Initiative (PACI) observed in 2006 that pastors of churches that the IRS had investigated based on referrals during the 2006 election cycle generally made conscious efforts to avoid express endorsements of candidates. Far more difficult are the issues to communications that convey a message on behalf of or in opposition to a candidate indirectly.

ELLEN P. APRILL

Political Campaign Intervention—
Indirect Endorsement or Opposition

The PACI Report pointed out that many churches and ministers believe that the political campaign intervention prohibition is limited to expressly endorsing or opposing candidates. Such is not the case. It applies as well to an indirect endorsement if it clearly conveys a message on behalf of, or in opposition to a candidate. Whether or not such activity violates the ban depends on the facts and circumstances. The possibility of indirect endorsement complicates compliance for synagogues and rabbis. By its very nature, it grants a degree of discretion to IRS agents in a particularly sensitive area of the law, one closely allied to precious First Amendment freedoms.

Facts-and-circumstances tests are commonplace throughout the law in general and tax law in particular. It is also standard practice to apply tax laws to both direct and indirect violations. To do otherwise would permit too easy an avoidance of the rules. Moreover, recent guidance from the IRS has gone a long way in clarifying what is and is not indirect endorsement or opposition.

Again, the Church Guide offers helpful examples of frequently encountered situations. The key question in each case is whether the activity at issue is conducted in a nonpartisan manner. Thus, a congregation may invite a candidate to speak as a candidate if the congregation gives the other candidates an equal opportunity to speak. In one example, each of three congressional candidates for the district in which a church is located were invited to speak on successive Sundays as part of regular worship services. Each answers questions on a wide variety of topics from the congregation. Such actions did not violate the political campaign intervention prohibition. In another example, only one candidate is invited. The candidate asks for the congregation's votes during the candidate's remarks. According to the IRS, such actions constitute violation of the political campaign intervention ban by the church.

In some cases, revenue-generating activities could constitute political campaign intervention. The Church Guide also offers examples of partisan and nonpartisan business activity. In the "good" example, a church rents its hall for a fee to a candidate for a fundraising dinner on the same first-come, first-served basis it has done for members of the public for several years. In the "bad" example, the church rents its mailing list, which it has never done before, to the campaign committee of a candidate who supports funding for faith-based programs and declines to rent its mailing list to the campaign committees of other candidates.

By far the most difficult line-drawing occurs when public policy discussion or issue advocacy could be viewed as indirect political campaign intervention. The Church Guide states, "Like other section 501(c)(3) organizations, some churches and religious organizations take positions on public policy issues, including issues that divide candidates in an election for public office. However, section 501(c)(3) organizations must avoid any issue advocacy that functions as political campaign intervention." The Church Guide lists key factors for determining whether a communication results in political campaign intervention. They are important enough to list in full.

- whether the statement identifies one or more candidates for a given public office,
- whether the statement expresses approval or disapproval for one or more candidates' positions and/or actions,
- whether the statement is delivered close in time to the election,
- whether the statement makes reference to voting or an election,
- whether the issue addressed in the communication has been raised as an issue distinguishing candidates for a given office,
- whether the communication is part of an ongoing series of communications by the organization on the same issue that are made independent of the timing of any election, and
- whether the timing of the communication and identification of the candidate are related to a non-electoral event such as a scheduled vote on specific legislation by an officeholder who also happens to be a candidate for public office.

The Church Guide cautions that although a communication must be considered in context, it is "particularly at risk of political campaign intervention when it makes reference to candidates or voting in a specific upcoming election."

The Church Guide includes a telling example, one that may be troubling to some, but worthy of careful consideration. In the example, Candidates A and B are running for state senate in a particular district. The issue of state funding for faith-based indigent hospital care in the district is a prominent issue in the campaign, and both candidates have spoken out on it. Candidate A supports such funding; Candidate B does not, supporting instead increased state funding for public hospitals. At the church's annual fundraising dinner, which takes place a month before the election, P, the head of a board of elders at a church in the district, gives a long speech about health care issues in which he discusses the issue of funding for faith-based programs. He does not name any candidate or political party. He makes the following statement at the end of the speech: "For those of you who care about quality of life in District W and the desire of our community for health care responsive to their faith, there is a very important choice coming up next month. We need more funding for health care. Increased public hospital funding will not make a difference. You have the power to respond to the needs of this community. Use that power when you go to the polls and cast your vote in the election for your state senator." The IRS concludes that the church has violated the political campaign intervention prohibition because the remarks of the church elder occurred at an official function, shortly before the election, and referred to an upcoming election after stating a position on an issue that is prominent in a campaign that distinguishes the candidates.

That the political campaign intervention prohibition applies to indirect endorsement requires heightened sensitivity on the part of rabbis. It does not mean that clergy need hesitate to remind congregants to get involved in the election and vote. It does not mean that, close to elections, rabbis need to cease discussion of public policy issues, even those issues that distinguish candidates. As the example above demonstrates, however, it does mean that policy discussions and "get out the vote" exhortations or any other reference to the election be separated rather than combined.

Although campaign intervention can occasionally take place without naming any candidate, the IRS guidelines specify that naming any candidate is a particularly important factor. They thus strongly suggest that rabbis and congregations avoid any discussion of candidates by name, unless done in a scrupulously nonpartisan manner. That is, any discussion of candidates by name should be such that a disinterested observer would not consider the communication as endorsing one of the candidates over another. An example of such a neutral presentation would be a forum in which a representative of each candidate presents that candidate's views. The political campaign intervention prohibition may also call for care in inviting guest speakers close to an election. Caution may counsel that clergy and lay leaders remind guests speaking on politically sensitive topics about these rules before they address the congregation.

With cautions such as these, rabbis and congregations will find themselves in little danger of violating the ban on intervention in campaigns for public office.

Results of the IRS Political Action Compliance Initiatives

As noted earlier, in recent election cycles, the IRS has conducted Political Activity Compliance Initiatives. Based on referrals, it examined possible political activity among some one hundred exempt organizations in each of the 2004, 2006, and 2008 election cycles. Results are available for 2004 and 2006. For both election cycles, the most common violations identified as being those of the forty-plus churches among those organizations selected for examination were distribution of printed documents supporting candidates, statements endorsing candidates during normal services, well-known individuals endorsing a candidate at an official church function, candidates speaking at official functions, and distributions of partisan voter guides.

Although the statutory prohibition by its terms is absolute such that even a de minimis amount of political campaign intervention could result in loss of exemption, the IRS did not revoke exemption in any of these cases. Neither did it impose the available excise tax of 10 percent on political campaign intervention expenditures. It instead issued written advisories because either the act of intervention was shown to be an anomaly or because the organization corrected the intervention and took steps to prevent future intervention.

Lobbying

Under the tax rules, communications that congregants understand to be policy discussions could be considered indirect endorsements that are impermissible political campaign interventions. In the case of lobbying, the misunderstanding often goes in the other direction—statements that congregants perceive to be impermissible political activity are likely to be perfectly permissible lobbying activity. Synagogues are permitted to lobby both legislators and the public to a certain extent. (Again, when clergy engage in lobbying communications at official functions or in official publications, such communications will be attributed to the congregation. Such communications are not forbidden but will count toward the amorphous limit.) As a practical matter, moreover, the limit on lobbying is seldom a concern in synagogue life.

In the language of the Internal Revenue Code, an organization is exempt under section 501(c)(3) so long as "no substantial part" of its activities consist of "carrying on propaganda, or otherwise attempting, to influence legislation." (The Internal Revenue Code permits most charities, but not churches, to elect to be subject to certain dollar limits up to $1 million, on a sliding scale depending on an organization's size, for lobbying expenditures.[6]) In *Regan v. Taxation with Representation of Washington*,[7] the Supreme Court upheld the limit on the ability of section 501(c)(3) organizations to lobby on the grounds that, since they received tax-deductible contributions, Congress can refuse to pay for lobbying activities "out of public moneys."

As various guidance from the IRS has explained,[8] legislation includes action by Congress, any state legislature, local governing bodies, and by the public in a referendum, ballot initiative, constitutional amendment, or similar procedure. It does not include actions by executive branch or independent administrative agencies or judicial bodies. Attempting to influence legislation includes direct contacts with legislators and their staffs to propose, support, or oppose legislation, as well as efforts to urge the general public to contact legislators or their staffs to propose, support, or oppose legislation. Neither policy discussion nor education is lobbying. Conveying nonpartisan analysis, study, or research on legislative matters to legislators is not lobbying, so long as such analysis is not intended to support a particular position. Communicating with members of the congregation on issues of common interest is not lobbying. If, however, members are urged to contact legislators or their staffs or members of the general public in support of or opposition to specific legislation, then lobbying is taking place.

Lobbying activities can lead to revocation of exemption only if they are a substantial part of the organization's activities, relative to its other activities. There is no clear guidance from the IRS or the courts as to what is substantial. A case in 1955 held that devoting less than 5 percent of an organization's time and effort to lobbying was insubstantial; a case in 1974 found activities in the 16 to 20 percent range to be substantial. Other cases have used a subjective balancing test involving all the facts and circumstances in which relevant factors include the percentage of an organization's budget (or employee time) spent on lobbying, the continuous or intermittent nature of the organization's legislative involvement, and the nature of the organization and its aims.[9] According to the Church Guide, the IRS "considers a variety of factors, including the time devoted (by both compensated and volunteer workers) and the expenditures devoted by the organization to the activity."

It is not unusual for clergy, congregational boards, or social action committees to urge their members, or pass resolutions urging their members or the public, to contact legislators regarding specific acts of legislation or to write such letters on behalf of the congregation. All such activity would constitute lobbying. But whatever test for substantiality is applied, it is unlikely that violations of the lobbying limitation would occur, given all the other activities of our congregations. Very occasionally, some additional caution may be prudent. The "substantial part" test does include volunteer efforts, and it can be difficult at times to know when an individual's activities should be attributed to the organization. Thus, in a situation similar to California's Proposition 8, which required marriage to be between a man and a woman, and which so many of our congregations so strongly and actively opposed, it may be useful for some congregations to keep records of when their members are acting in their capacity as synagogue members as well as what other synagogue resources are being devoted to the lobbying effort. With such records, they would be prepared in the unlikely event of any challenge, whether from the IRS, the press, or the blogosphere.

Conclusion

When it comes to synagogue involvement in the political process and eligibility for tax exemption, the Internal Revenue Code has different rules for different kinds of activities. It forbids all intervention on behalf of or in opposition to the political campaign of any candidate for public office. As a rule of thumb, rabbis and others in congregational life will avoid violating this prohibition in the vast majority of cases if they avoid discussing candidates by name. They are always free to engage in discussions of public policy, although they need to exercise care and sensitivity in discussing particular policy issues that distinguish candidates for a particular office close to an election. Lobbying, in contrast, is not forbidden. Synagogues may support or oppose legislation so long as such lobbying does not constitute a "substantial part" of a congregation's activities. This limit is unlikely to pose a problem in any but the very most unusual cases. Thus, while rabbis face many challenges in deciding what role politics should play in their rabbinates, complying with the strictures of the Internal Revenue Code should not pose a significant burden.

References

IRS Tax Guide for Churches and Religious Organizations (major resource discussed herein)
http://www.irs.gov/pub/irs-pdf/p1828.pdf

Political Activity Guidelines for Catholic Organizations (detailed multi-entry guidelines and discussion)
http://www.usccb.org/ogc/guidelines.shtml

Politics and Pulpit 2008: A Guide to the Internal Revenue Code Restrictions on the Political Activity of Religious Organizations (Pew Forum on Religion and Public Life)
http://pewforum.org/newassets/misc/politics_and_the_pulpit_2008.pdf

Revenue Ruling 2007-41 (precedential guidance on which Church Guide is based)
http://www.irs.gov/irb/2007-25_IRB/ar09.html

Speak Truth to Power: A Guide for Congregations Taking Public Policy Positions (URJ)
http://urj.org//cong/board//?syspage=document&item_id=14873

Notes

1. H.R. Rep. No. 100-391 (II), at 1625, 1627 (1987).
2. *Branch Ministries v. Rossotti*, 211 F.3d 137 (D.C. Cir. 2000).

3. See ADF Web site at http://www.adfmedia.org/News/PRDetail/9835?search=1.
4. Such public guidance includes regulations, which represent the most authoritative guidance, and revenue rulings, which represent the official interpretation of the IRS on matters of law arising in particular factual settings as well as other less authoritative forms of guidance, such as technical advice memoranda and notices. See Treas. Reg. sec. 1.501(c)(3)-1(c)(3)(iii); Rev. Rul. 67-71, 1967-1 C.B. 125; Tech. Adv. Mem. 9130008, and Notice 89-76, 1988-2 C.B. 392.
5. Rev. Rul. 2007-41, 2007-1 C.B. 1421. The examples in the Tax Guide for Churches are closely based on those in Rev. Rul. 2007-41. This essay does not discuss all of the many examples in the Tax Guide.
6. Major religious organizations asked, apparently on what they saw as constitutional grounds, not to be subject to any such limitation at the time this election was enacted.
7. *Regan v. Taxation with Representation of Washington,* 461 U.S. 540 (1983).
8. Authorities include Treas. Reg. sec. 1.501(c)(3)-1(c)(3)(ii); Rev. Rul. 70-79, 1970-1 C.B. 127; and Rev. Rul. 70-449, 1970-2 C.B. 111.
9. See *Seasongood v. Commissioner,* 227 F.2d 907 (6th Cir. 1955) **(less than 5% insubstantial)**; *Haswell v. United States,* 500 F.2d 1133 (Ct. Cl. 1974), *cert. denied* 419 U.S. 1107 (1975) **(16–20% in context of balancing test; insubstantial)**; *Christian Echoes National Ministry, Inc. v. United States,* 470 F.2d 849 (10th Cir. 1972) **(applying balancing test to find lobbying violation)**.

Liberal Dilemma: The Prophetic Mandate versus Religion-State Separation in Reform Political Discourse

A. Brian Stoller

I. Introduction

Is Reform Judaism's religious commitment to speaking truth to power in the tradition of the prophets compatible with its resolve to maintain a separation between religion and state? Or, in upholding the one principle, do we necessarily violate the other?

On various occasions, official organs of the Reform Movement have adopted resolutions outlining Jewish teachings on a particular political issue and publicly calling on the U.S. and Canadian governments to implement specific policies on the basis of those teachings. With one such resolution dealing with energy and climate change having recently been passed by the 2009 URJ biennial convention, now is an opportune moment to evaluate whether the URJ's approach to secular political discourse via its public-policy resolutions is consistent with (1) the principles that characterize public discourse in an open, liberal society, and (2) the ideal of religion-state separation—both being values to which the Reform Movement professes fealty.

The basis for this discussion will be a 2007 URJ Executive Committee resolution calling on the U.S. government to set a timetable for withdrawing U.S. forces from Iraq. In arguing why withdrawal is necessary, the resolution contends that the U.S. government has failed to meet certain standards required by the Jewish laws of war (*hilchot milchamah*). This approach to public advocacy invites

---

A. BRIAN STOLLER (C08) is assistant rabbi at Congregation B'nai Jehoshua Beth Elohim in Deerfield, Illinois. Prior to entering HUCJIR, he served from 1999–2003 as an aide to then-U.S. Senator Peter G. Fitzgerald of Illinois.

questions about the appropriateness of such religious discourse in the public sphere.

In exploring these questions, this article will first review the relevant sections of the 2007 resolution and discuss the implications of the URJ's stated aim to effect government policy changes, via the resolution, explicitly on the basis of Jewish teachings. From there, it will proceed to evaluate the resolution against two discrete philosophical models for liberal public discourse, in order to discern what the URJ Iraq War resolution suggests about the Reform Movement's perspective on religious argumentation in the public sphere. It will conclude by offering recommendations for addressing what seems to be Reform Judaism's "liberal dilemma," which arises from the way in which the Movement tends to understand (1) the prophetic mandate and (2) potential threats to religion-state separation.

II. URJ Resolution on the War in Iraq, 2007

On January 10, 2007, President George W. Bush announced that the United States would deploy more than twenty thousand additional troops to Iraq. The president's announcement prompted the Reform Movement, which had previously taken public positions on the Iraq war on at least three separate occasions, to speak out once again on the issue, this time in opposition to the new "surge" strategy. The URJ Executive Committee adopted a resolution on March 12, 2007, calling on President Bush and Congress to oppose increasing the number of U.S. troops deployed in Iraq and to set a timetable for withdrawing U.S. forces from that country. In addition to the rising number of U.S. casualties and the burgeoning financial cost of the war, the URJ resolution cites, as a reason why withdrawal is necessary, the "significant abuses and failures of Jewish just war standards"[1]—i.e., *hilchot milchamah*, as the resolution defines them—perpetrated by the U.S. government. This assertion that the U.S. government should adhere to halachic standards is, of course, problematic. Before exploring that issue in detail, however, it is first necessary to survey, in relatively brief fashion, the resolution's use of religious argumentation in calling for withdrawal from Iraq.

A. Religious Argumentation in the URJ Resolution

The resolution consists of an action section, in which it calls on the president and Congress to oppose troop increases and to set a withdrawal timetable, and five background sections (Sections I–V) explaining the reasons for its position. Of primary interest to this analysis is Section III, entitled "Jewish Values Regarding Rules of War." This section makes a series of critiques of U.S. policy on the basis of specifically Jewish arguments. In Section IV, the resolution provides additional policy critiques that are not based on religious arguments; however, it must be emphasized that it is the incorporation of Jewish textual citations in Section III that gives the resolution a Jewish character and imputes it with a measure of religious authority, lending sanction from the tradition to the resolution's nonreligious arguments.

As noted above, the basis for the resolution's religious argumentation is *hilchot milchamah*, the Jewish laws of war. It is exclusively within the framework of this discrete legal institution that the halachic state is permitted to wage war. *Hilchot milchamah* identify two categories of permissible war: *milchemet mitzvah* (war that is commanded explicitly by the Torah, such as the conquest of Amalek and the Seven Nations that occupied Canaan, as well as the rabbinically sanctioned defensive war in response to enemy aggression) and *milchemet hareshut* (discretionary war, such as a war of expansion and a war to magnify the king's greatness and reputation).[2] To prevent the Jewish state from acting recklessly, *hilchot milchamah* require it to follow strict guidelines in the initiation and conduct of war. While much deserves to be said about the fact that the normative halachic tradition limits the application of *hilchot milchamah* to a Jewish state governed by a king and/or the Great Sanhedrin, which must obtain divine authorization for war either from the Torah or via the *urim* and *tumim* (the oracles on the High Priest's breastplate), such a discussion is beyond the scope of this article. For purposes of the present discussion, it is sufficient to note that the URJ resolution reinterprets the halachic rubric in order to apply it to modern U.S. and international institutions and uses it as a paradigm for evaluating the legitimacy of the Iraq war.[3]

On the basis of its particular interpretation of *hilchot milchamah*, the resolution deems war waged to forestall a distant threat to be a form of discretionary war. It is this latter category which is relevant to the resolution's analysis of the Iraq war. After stating definitively that Jewish tradition would categorize the Iraq war as *milchemet hareshut*, the resolution asserts that

The clear evidence of the 9/11 Commission that Saddam was not close to developing or obtaining nuclear or biological weapons, that his chemical weapon capacity was almost entirely eliminated, and that he did not cooperate with Al Qaeda in attacks on the U.S., mitigates any arguments of imminence.[4]

Given the resolution's prior contention that the only justifiable anticipatory wars are those waged when there is clear evidence of an imminent threat, this statement paves the way (1) for the resolution to claim that the Iraq war is unjustifiable in the eyes of Jewish tradition and (2) to call for withdrawal on that basis.

Noting that, in comparison to *milchamot mitzvah*, *milchamot hareshut* "have stricter requirements in terms of right authority and just means,"[5] the resolution proceeds to apply its particular interpretations of those requirements to the Iraq war. First, it notes that *hilchot milchamah* require the Jewish king to obtain approval from the Sanhedrin for *milchemet hareshut*. Then, equating the halachic monarch and Sanhedrin with modern U.S. institutions, the resolution cites this authorization requirement as the basis for its view, espoused in the URJ's 2002 position statement, that the U.S. president must obtain congressional approval before sending troops into Iraq.[6] Furthermore, it maintains that

> in our contemporary world, there is a strong argument that "right authority" for international intervention requires legitimate international authority—something the U.S. recognized in bringing its case to the U.N. But the lack of support from the U.N. Security Council and NATO denied that right authority.[7]

To wit, according to the resolution, Jewish law required the U.S. government to have obtained UN and NATO approval before commencing military action against Iraq. The citation of the halachic authorization requirement thus provides religiously authoritative support for the resolution's argument that the U.S. war in Iraq was initiated improperly and should therefore be discontinued.

Next, the resolution notes that *hilchot milchamah* require the Jewish state to offer the enemy peace before initiating war: "The halachah is clear about the need to pursue vigorously peaceful options before the use of force could be justified (Maimonides, *Mishneh Torah, Melachim* 6:1)."[8] This statement implies quite strongly that Jewish tradition mandates the U.S. government seek a peaceful resolution to the conflict with Iraq and that war must be a last resort. The parenthetical citation of the *Mishneh Torah* provides religious substantiation for the resolution's argument that the Iraq war is unjustified in part because the 9/11 Commission determined that the United States had failed to pursue all reasonable peaceful solutions before initiating military action.

The document goes on to explain that, according to Maimonides, the Talmudic principle of *bal tashchit* requires that

> war should be fought in a manner so as to allow normal civilian life to resume after the war...Fighting wars in a way that allows for the return to peace and normal life must always be the goal.[9]

The resolution further asserts that

> Central to Jewish just means doctrine is the need to protect innocent civilians (MT *Melachim* 6:11 [sic]).[10] The alarming devastation wrought [in Iraq] has been damaging for the civilian population.[11]

Once again, this invocation of Jewish law lends religious authority to the resolution's argument that the war in Iraq is unjust in part because so many civilians have been harmed or killed during the operation. In each of these instances, the resolution's use of religious language and reasoning to substantiate its arguments against the Iraq war is plainly evident.

B. The Aims of the Resolution

The URJ resolution explicitly outlines its objectives and aggressively seeks to impact secular society. Articulating its *raison d'être* in the introductory section, the resolution states that the Reform Movement has spoken out on the Iraq war in the past and chooses to do so again because

> the prophetic tradition, so central to Judaism, calls on us to address the great moral issues of our day. And no issue raises more urgent and challenging moral considerations for our nations [i.e., the United States and Canada]...than does the war in Iraq.[12]

In the press release announcing the resolution's adoption, then-URJ Board of Trustees Chairman Robert Heller echoes this statement of purpose, asserting that the Movement passed the resolution "in keeping with our prophetic obligation to speak truth to power."[13] These statements demonstrate quite clearly that the Reform Movement sees it as its religious duty not only to bring Jewish values, as it understands them, to bear on matters of public debate, but also to do so publicly, in the manner of the prophets. To wit, the resolution is written not as an intellectual exercise or to satisfy the spiritual needs of Reform Jews, but, rather, to raise a social critique in the public sphere and move those in power to act.

Lest this intention be in doubt, the resolution addresses the U.S. and Canadian governments directly, imploring them to implement certain policies on the basis of the resolution's arguments. In the concluding section, the document calls on President Bush and Congress to

> Set and announce a clear timetable for the phased and expeditious withdrawal of United States troops from Iraq [and to] [i]nclude the estimated cost of the war in the annual budget and not through emergency supplemental bills.[14]

The resolution further calls upon both national governments and the international community to

> Encourage Iraq Prime Minister Nuri Kamal al-Maliki to resume reconciliation talks with the full range of Iraq's political leaders [and to] [a]ctively support a dialogue between Iraq and all its neighbors, especially in regards to helping to stop civil strife and terrorism and helping finance Iraqi job programs and reconstruction.[15]

Though many U.S. and international policy-oriented groups have pressed the government to take similar actions, the obvious questions in regard to the URJ resolution are: what particular standing does a religious organization have to speak about national security policy and why should its recommendations be heeded?[16] While the URJ could attempt to demonstrate its credibility to speak about the issue by basing its critiques on secular news sources, government reports, and other similar material, the use of classical Jewish text may be more effective in this regard. Using *hilchot milchamah* in its resolution—instead of, or in conjunction with, secular sources—has the important effect of giving the URJ's secular policy arguments a distinctive religious character and authority. This, in turn, makes the arguments appear credible coming from a religious organization.

This use of *hilchot milchamah* has an additional and consequential effect: By injecting arguments of this nature into the public sphere, the resolution necessarily brings the values and teachings of a particular religious tradition to bear on the workings of secular government and society. On the one hand, the resolution indicates that it intends to do precisely that in accordance with its prophetic responsibility. On the other hand, the Reform Movement, which terms its brand of religion "liberal Judaism," professes a strong and sincere commitment to the separation of religion and state. To reiterate the question posed at the beginning of this article: Are these two values, as the Reform Movement understands them, compatible? In attempting to answer that question, it is helpful to consider some ideas from academic political philosophy regarding the bounds of proper discourse in a liberal society such as the United States.

III. Political Liberalism and Models of Liberal Discourse

"Liberalism" is an umbrella term encompassing various schools of political philosophy that envision a society in which each individual citizen can freely pursue his own ends without others seeking to impose upon him a conception of "the good life" (or "the good"). To safeguard against coercion that undermines such freedom, liberalism insists that public discourse in a liberal society must take place within certain rhetorical boundaries, which exist in principle if not in law. However, the precise contours of those boundaries, which determine those forms of language and argumentation that are appropriate for the public sphere and those forms that are inappropriate, is a point of debate among liberal philosophers.

One key issue of contention is the propriety of religious argumentation in public discourse. Because a religion advances a particular notion of the good that is based on a belief system not shared by non-adherents, some liberal thinkers maintain that religious argumentation in the public sphere constitutes an undue imposition of a particular idea of the good on non-believing citizens. Others, by contrast, hold that barring religious discourse from the public sphere undermines what should be the overarching aims of the liberal society.

In order to facilitate an assessment of the URJ resolution in light of principles of liberalism, it is helpful to outline the broad concepts of classical liberal theory and then consider, in relative brevity, two distinct philosophical models of liberal society: (1) Michael Sandel's communitarianism, which rejects certain key premises of the classical model; and (2) Ronald Dworkin's "integrated community" model, which aims to incorporate communitarian elements into a modified version of the classical paradigm.

A. Classical Liberalism: An Overview

The concept of justice is essential to classical liberal theory. According to the classical view, the only just society is the one that protects each individual citizen's freedom to pursue his own idea of the good without interference or coercion by other citizens or the state. In order to facilitate an environment in which such freedom can exist, society must adopt a governing concept of justice that is prior to the good; that is to say, the governing justice concept must be blind to, and uninfluenced by, citizens' particular desires and biases. If this is not the case—i.e., if the governing justice concept is not *prior* to the good but, rather, *influenced* by one or more particular ideas of the good espoused by societal members—then that justice concept would necessarily infringe on the freedom of citizens who do not share those ideas. In a word, such a society would not be truly just.

John Rawls, the twentieth-century Harvard University political philosopher and renowned exponent of liberal political theory, contends that justice must be founded in something that is external to the human self. Rawls argues that society should be organized on the basis of what he calls "the original position." This model requires citizens to determine society's governing principles from behind a "veil of ignorance," meaning that they must approach the task by acting as though they do not know what their respective lots in society might be; that is to say, they should make decisions about societal justice as if they do not know whether, once they move from this "original position" to a real position in society, they would be wealthy or poor, healthy or sickly, white or black. Rawls terms this ideal decision-maker the "unencumbered self," which Sandel describes as "a self understood as prior to and independent of purposes and ends."[17] Rawls maintains that this process alone can produce a justice concept that does not presuppose any idea of "the good." This objective justice concept would then be enshrined in the laws and political procedures of the liberal state, which, according to classical liberal theory, functions primarily to protect each citizen's unfettered right to pursue his own idea of the good. The classical liberal model envisions each individual as an isolated atom; one individual's freedom ends where another's begins.

B. Michael Sandel: A Communitarian Model

In his article "The Procedural Republic and the Unencumbered Self," Michael Sandel, a contemporary political philosopher and Harvard University government professor, rejects the Rawlsian model of liberalism, contending that it is unrealistic; human beings, he argues, can never attain the ideal of the unencumbered self. Sandel explains that while the individual's various experiences and communal attachments—e.g., familial, religious, national, and ethnic—constitute the essence of who he is as a human being, "the liberal ethic puts the self beyond the reach of its experience, beyond deliberation and reflection."[18] That is to say, the liberal insistence that the individual must sever himself from his identity and stand behind a veil of ignorance in order to participate in public discourse is not only fanciful, but alienating as well. The crux of Sandel's argument is that classical atomistic liberalism suppresses the aspects of humanity that, if embraced, could contribute to the creation of a healthy society.

Moreover, he contends that, in its zealous concern for protecting each citizen's right to pursue his own ends, classical liberalism fosters isolated individualism at the expense of community. Though citizens interact regularly with each other on a nonpolitical level, their interactions in public discourse, in accordance with liberalism's narrowly defined boundaries, occur only through the laws and institutions of the liberal state. This "procedural republic," as Sandel terms the liberal society in practice, undermines both community and democracy.

Sandel, therefore, proposes an alternative to classical liberalism. Rather than organize society around an unrealistic notion of justice that is untouched by any particular concept of "the good," he envisions a communitarian society and discourse that embraces its citizens' diverse experiences, identities, and visions of the good life. Rather than idealize the unencumbered self, who checks his humanity at the door, Sandel's communitarian society would invite each citizen to bring his particular idea of the good to the public arena and subject it to the marketplace of ideas. By relating to their fellow citizens as whole persons from whom they can learn, rather than as distant individuals from whom they need protection, societal members could draw on diverse viewpoints in a collective effort to create the best possible community. In short, Sandel's communitarian society is concerned primarily not with the individual's right to pursue his own ends but, rather, with the community's right to pursue the common good.

C. Ronald Dworkin: The Integrated Community

Ronald Dworkin, another leading contemporary political philosopher and New York University law professor, likewise recognizes that individuals' various experiences and communal associations shape who they are as human beings and that severing themselves completely from those attachments is both unrealistic and undesirable. Unlike Sandel, however, Dworkin rejects the communitarian contention that liberalism is incompatible with community. He maintains that, on the contrary, communitarian discourse can flourish only in a society that preserves liberal rights. Dworkin argues that "liberalism supplies the best interpretation of [a certain] concept of community,"[19] which he calls the "integrated community."

The integrated community model allows for communitarian discourse within the bounds of a liberal framework. In this model, citizens recognize that "the lives of individual people and that of their community are integrated, and that the critical success of any one of their lives is an aspect of, and so is dependent on, the goodness of the community as a whole."[20] Therefore integrated citizens—or "civic republicans," as Dworkin terms them—act both individually and collectively to advance the good of the community. As in the communitarian model, the community is prior to the individual.

For Dworkin, the community is an entity defined by the particular practices in which it collectively engages. The community's idea of the good is defined by the community as a whole, in terms accessible to, and agreed upon by, every member. Individuals associate with the integrated community voluntarily because they share with the community some common sense of "the good." In the integrated community model, the civic republican advocates for his conception of the good only as it relates to relevant communal acts; when members' actions do not bear directly on communal acts, he respects their boundaries. Promoting a vision of the good that is not directly relevant to the community's practice transgresses the bounds of acceptable discourse.

To illustrate his hybrid liberal-communitarian model, Dworkin brings the example of an orchestra. An orchestra's communal act is the production of music, and the community's idea of the good, all members can agree, is to maximize the quality of music that the orchestra produces. Within this integrated community, members may advocate for their ideas of the good insofar as those ideas advance the *communal* good. For example, one violinist may urge another to purchase a more expensive bow, which he believes enhances sound quality. Even if the violinist receiving the counsel disagrees and chooses not to accept it, the advice is nevertheless legitimate discourse because it relates to the communal acts of the orchestra. If, on the other hand, the violinist urges his colleague to eat less red meat in order to reduce his cholesterol, his advice is inappropriate. In promoting his own conception of the good on this matter, the violinist may believe he is aiding the well-being of his colleague; however, because the advice does not relate to the practices of the integrated community, it is illiberal discourse according to the Dworkin model.

In sum, Dworkin envisions a society in which communitarian discourse is possible within clearly defined boundaries. Participants in political discourse must be conscious of the nature of their community. While Dworkin allows individuals the freedom to draw on their experiences and unique identities in advocating for the good within the integrated community, he contends that such advocacy is permissible only with regard to the particular acts that define the community. Moreover, it must be presented in terms that are accessible to all community members.

IV. The URJ Resolution as a Functionary in American Public Discourse

As discussed above, the URJ resolution evidently seeks not only to influence the internal Reform community, but also to make an impact upon secular American society. It therefore must be regarded as functioning, at least in part, within the realm of American political discourse. As such, it is possible to apply the Dworkin and Sandel paradigms in order to discern which model of discourse the resolution more closely represents. This, in turn, may shed light on the relationship between religion and the public sphere in Reform culture. This is a potentially informative exercise, given the Reform Movement's longstanding emphasis on the necessity of a clear separation between religion and state in American society.

A. The American Political Community: Its Nature, Communal Acts, and Idea of the Good

In order to assess the resolution in light of the Dworkin and Sandel models, it is first necessary to say something about the nature of the American political community in which it functions. Both philosophers agree that the United States is organized as a liberal society. The Declaration of Independence famously asserts that

> all men are created equal, that they are endowed by their Creator with certain unalienable Rights, that among these are Life, Liberty and the pursuit of Happiness.—That to secure these rights, Governments are instituted among Men, deriving their just powers from the consent of the governed...

This foundational statement suggests that the state's *raison d'être* is to guarantee every individual citizen's right to pursue his own ends without interference from others. This mission is enshrined in the nation's laws, which mediate all formal public interactions among the citizenry. While Sandel laments that this "procedural republic" form of societal organization suppresses the individual and undermines community in America,[21] Dworkin maintains that American political society has the characteristics of an "integrated community," in which community can flourish within appropriately defined parameters of discourse.

On Dworkin's model, the nature of proper discourse in a liberal society is determined according to five factors: (1) the nature of the community, (2) the communal acts that define the community, (3) how constituent members participate in communal acts, (4) its communal idea of the good, and (5) the communal vocabulary of discourse. Dworkin explains that the communal acts of the American political community are "the acts of its government through its legislative, executive, and judicial decisions," and that the community is "composed of those who play some role in those decisions and who are most directly affected by them."[22] All communal acts—both by the government as communal agent and by individual public citizens as communal members—should serve the communal idea of the good, which, as articulated by the Preamble to the Constitution, is "to form a more perfect union, establish justice, insure domestic tranquility, provide for the common defense, promote the general welfare, and secure the blessings of liberty to ourselves and our posterity...." To illustrate how the American political community functions according to Dworkin's integrated community framework, it is helpful to return to the example of the orchestra:

1. **The nature of the community.** Whereas the orchestra is comprised of musicians, the American political community is comprised of individual public citizens.
2. **The communal act(s).** Whereas the orchestra's communal act is producing music, the American political community's communal acts are those taken by its government.
3. **Constituent members' participation in the communal act(s).** Whereas the orchestra's musicians participate in the communal act by playing their instruments, America's public citizens participate in the communal acts by voting and advocating in the public sphere.
4. **The communal idea of the good.** Whereas the orchestra's communal idea of the good is to maximize the quality of the music it produces, the American political community's idea of the good is to realize the vision articulated by the Constitution.
5. **The communal vocabulary of discourse.** Whereas the orchestral community speaks in commonly accessible terms relating to music, the American political community speaks in commonly accessible terms relating to public policy.

B. The URJ Resolution's Idea of the Good and the Nature of its Discourse

As noted previously, the URJ resolution occasionally argues on secular grounds for withdrawal from Iraq. For example, in Section IV it states that

> Notwithstanding limited progress, the level of sectarian violence and casualties, both Iraqi and American has risen sharply.... In addition to the human cost of the war, the economic price of the war continues to divert much-needed funds away from domestic U.S. concerns.... [This] will require future generations to pay the cost as a result of concurrent tax cuts coupled with spending of substantial levels of borrowed funds.... A wide array of military and policy experts have pointed out that the financial burden also diminishes the ability of the U.S. military to respond to other threats and acts as a barrier to U.S. cooperation with the international community on other issues.[23]

If, in the context of war and foreign policy, it is possible to conceive of the communal idea of the good as the promotion of a safe, fiscally healthy, and internationally effective United States, then it is reasonable to conclude that the above arguments are rooted in that vision. In this passage, the resolution urges the United States to withdraw its forces from Iraq because the prospects of risking the further loss of life, spending more money in a futile fight, weakening U.S. defense capabilities, and diminishing its standing abroad, undermines, rather than advances, the interests of the state. While it is possible for citizens to disagree with the resolution's arguments, the important point is that the arguments are articulated in the American political community's common vocabulary. Therefore, all community members can relate to these arguments and debate their merits in the public sphere.

In Dworkin's integrated community model, it will be recalled, appropriate public discourse is only that which (1) relates to the practices that define the community, (2) promotes the communal idea of the good, and (3) utilizes the common parlance so as to be accessible to all members. The resolution's argumentation in the above passage (and throughout Section IV) is consistent with these criteria. As such, the advancement of these arguments in the public sphere, through the publication of this resolution, constitutes, in Dworkin's terms, an act of "civic republicanism" by the URJ. To wit, these arguments, taken alone, are appropriate to liberal public discourse according to Dworkin's integrated community model.

Complications arise, however, because the arguments in Section IV cannot be taken alone; they exist, rather, in the broader context of a resolution, which, as outlined previously, uses extensive religious argumentation to make its case. Indeed, it is arguably the religious language that gives the resolution its force. As already discussed, the URJ, as a religious organization, has no credibility to make national security arguments *qua* national security arguments in the public sphere; though it may certainly try, government officials would have no reason to heed such arguments coming from an organization whose specialty is religion rather than foreign policy. The resolution can be credible only insofar as it frames its arguments in terms of the URJ's particular area of expertise. The specifically Jewish argumentation in Section III, therefore, is the linchpin of the resolution in that it serves (in appearance if not in actuality) to justify *all* of the document's assertions, even those that do not directly reference Jewish teachings. In short, since the resolution's ability to impact secular society stems from its religious argumentation, the particular conception of the good articulated in that section is of primary concern.

It has already been shown how the resolution interprets *hilchot milchamah* to make the rubric relevant to the Iraq war and to establish distinctly Jewish grounds for its policy positions. Through its presentation of the halachic paradigm, the resolution informs its readers that Judaism (1) considers the Iraq war to be a war of choice rather than a war of necessity, (2) requires congressional approval for a war of this kind, (3) mandates that the United States pursue peaceful solutions to the conflict on its own and through international institutions before initiating war, and (4) requires that the United States army adequately preserve the Iraqi environment and infrastructure and minimize casualties among innocent civilians during combat. By using its perceived religious authority to establish these particular parameters for evaluating the actions of the U.S. government, the resolution embarks on a critique of the Iraq war that is based not on the American political community's idea of the good, but, rather, on a distinctly *Jewish* vision of the good.

The resolution pursues this line of critique overtly and aggressively, arguing for withdrawal from Iraq on unambiguously religious grounds. As noted above, the resolution asserts that because, according to its interpretation of the 9/11 Commission's report, the threat posed by Iraq was not an imminent one, the war must be conducted in accordance with the requirements governing the halachic category of *milchemet hareshut*. As such, the resolution maintains, Jewish tradition requires not only congressional authorization for war, but also "vigorous and effective Congressional oversight of the way the war has been prosecutedy...something that has been *woefully lacking* [emphasis added]."[24] Similarly, after explaining that "the halachah is clear about the need to pursue vigorously peaceful options before the use of force could be justified," the resolution goes on to contend that "This was a requirement that the 2002 URJ Executive committee decision called for and one that the 9/11 Commission found we had *failed to achieve* [emphasis added]."[25]

While the arguments that Congress has failed to provide adequate oversight and that the Bush Administration rushed into war before exhausting all diplomatic solutions are commonplace in the public sphere, what is unusual and remarkable here is the resolution's particular rationale for these criticisms: whereas those who make such arguments tend to condemn Congress and the Bush Administration for causing the needless loss of lives, taxpayer money, and international goodwill toward the United States, the resolution condemns the government for failing to meet the standards of *hilchot milchamah*. This line of argumentation is rooted in the premise that halachah, as the URJ interprets it, is the ultimate expression of the good; as such, the resolution implies, not so subtly, that the aim of the American political community—and of the government, as the agent of communal action—should be to adhere to the Reform Movement's particular understanding of Jewish law.

In the same vein, after explaining that Maimonides' exposition of the *bal tashchit* principle requires "that war should be fought in a manner so as to allow normal civilian life to resume after the war," the resolution goes on to contend that

> The failure of the U.S. government to secure the civilian infrastructure in the aftermath of the successful invasion and the failure in the following three years to rebuild effectively *ignores these values* [emphasis added] and is cited as a major failure in our limited success by the Baker-Hamilton Report.[26]

Here, too, the resolution casts its particular interpretation of halachah as the consummate measure of the good. While the criticism of the U.S. failure to rebuild Iraq's infrastructure is one that is also raised by secular critics, including the Baker-Hamilton Commission, the resolution makes this critique for a decidedly different reason: whereas others contend that this failure harms U.S. security and national interests, the resolution condemns it as a violation of *hilchot milchamah*, as the URJ interprets the rubric. The document makes this reasoning all the more explicit at the end of Section III, stating that

> In conclusion, our failure to pursue all reasonable alternatives to war, to mobilize the kind of broad-based international cooperation we had in the first Gulf War, the array of faulty justifications for war offered, the woeful lack of planning for the aftermath of the invasion, the disgraceful failure to protect the civilian infrastructure (*bal tashchit*), the abuses of prisoners, the alarming devastation wrought on civilians—all these and more raise significant abuses and failures of Jewish just war standards.[27]

As this statement indicates quite clearly, the resolution urges the president and Congress to oppose the troop "surge" and to set a timetable for withdrawing U.S. forces from Iraq in large part because, in initiating and conducting the war, the U.S. government has repeatedly violated halachah. In short, the resolution brings a particular Jewish conception of the good to bear in the sphere of American public discourse, and contends that the pursuit of that good necessitates withdrawal from Iraq.

By suggesting that a U.S. war can be justifiable only if it meets the halachic criteria as the URJ presents them, the resolution violates the boundaries of liberal discourse as Dworkin's integrated community model defines them. The idea of the good that it advocates, i.e., adherence to a Reform interpretation of halachah, relates neither to the American political community's defining communal practices nor to its common conception of the good; indeed, following Jewish law has never been an express aim of the American political community. Moreover, because the resolution uses particular Jewish language that is inaccessible to non-Jewish citizens, rather than the common vocabulary of communal discourse, its arguments cannot be dissected and debated by all participants in the public arena. By contending that the U.S. government should initiate and conduct the Iraq war in accordance with the standards of *hilchot milchamah*, the resolution equates its own Jewish vision of the good with the good of the community as a whole; and by promoting this particular religious idea of the good in the realm of general public discourse, the resolution's advocacy constitutes illiberal discourse according to the Dworkin model.

By contrast, Sandel's communitarian model does not insist that, in order to participate in public discourse, an organization must ground its arguments in a commonly accepted idea of the good. On the contrary, the Sandel model encourages individuals and groups to bring their own particular conceptions of the good, formed by their unique experiences and communal identifications, to the realm of public discourse. Rather than undermining freedom, such diversity of voices and viewpoints, Sandel maintains, contributes to the betterment of society. The resolution embodies this communitarian approach to discourse. By using halachic texts, as opposed to secular sources, to evaluate the justifiability of the Iraq war, it suggests that the Reform community cannot, and need not divorce itself from Judaism or the idea of the good that flows from it. Rather than attempt to participate in public debate over the war as some mythical unencumbered self, the URJ presents its particular conception of the good for scrutiny and discussion in the marketplace of ideas—believing, presumably, that the intellectual and emotional force of its arguments will persuade the majority of their virtue. Considered in the context of Sandel's model, this form of communitarian discourse is entirely appropriate for the public arena.

V. Communitarianism versus the Integrated Community: A Tension in Reform Discourse

To summarize, the URJ resolution seeks to impact the American political community by advocating in the public sphere for specific Iraq war policies on the basis of a particular Jewish conception of the good. By using *hilchot milchamah* to frame its arguments as distinctly religious, the URJ establishes its authority, as a religious organization, to weigh in on national security matters, on which it otherwise would not be viewed as a credible commentator. Moreover, by citing the halachic material, the resolution conveys the impression that its policy positions flow not from the authors' personal political views but, rather, from an authoritative religious tradition. Finally, in its use of specifically Jewish arguments to support a call for withdrawal from Iraq, the resolution embodies a communitarian approach to public discourse.

As noted above, the resolution explains that its purpose in critiquing the Iraq war is to meet its prophetic responsibility to speak out on the pressing moral issues of the day. How, then, does this communitarian impulse square with the Reform Movement's avowed commitment to the separation of religion and state? Evidence exists that the Reform Movement is aware of this tension between these two values in the abstract, although it is not necessarily conscious of the fact that the same tension exists in relation to the Movement's own discourse and actions.

On the one hand, the Reform Movement overtly espouses communitarianism, at least with regard to itself. For example, the CCAR's 1937 statement "The Guiding Principles of Reform Judaism," commonly known as the Columbus Platform, avers that "Judaism seeks the attainment of a just society by the application of its teachings to the economic order, to industry and commerce, and to national and international affairs."[28] The organization's platforms of 1885, 1976, and 1999 contain similar declarations, and the URJ Web site presently notes that "the Union has not hesitated to speak out on issues of the widest scope and significance, always seeking to elucidate current problems according to its interpretation of the voice of prophetic Judaism,"[29] a task which the resolution evidently pursues. Such statements indicate quite clearly that the Reform Movement aims, without reservation, to bring its particular Jewish idea of the good to bear in the public sphere. Indeed, current URJ president Rabbi Eric Yoffie recently explained that the Religious Action Center of Reform Judaism (RAC), the Movement's political advocacy arm, exists "to influence Congress on the greatest moral issues about which our Movement had spoken...."[30]

All of this would seem to run counter to the Reform Movement's contention that a strong separation between religion and state is essential in order to ensure "the protection of religion from government and the protection of government from religion."[31] In an implicit defense of the Movement's communitarian disposition, Rabbi Marla Feldman, chairwoman of the Movement's Commission on Social Action, maintains that

> The idea that people of faith have a mandate to bring their values into the public arena is not unique to the Reform Movement. There is a long tradition of faith groups "speaking truth to power" and advocating for social change, and every major religious organization in American life participates in this exercise. Religious voices have been central in the major social justice movements

throughout our nation's history, from the abolitionist movement to those involved with desegregation and civil rights. In the international arena as well, faith groups have led the way in advocating for nuclear disarmament, international aid and human rights around the world.[32]

Feldman's claim of a mandate for religious groups "to bring their values into the public arena" echoes Sandel, who maintains that such discourse fosters community and strengthens society. However, while Feldman touts various religious groups' key role in certain progressive political achievements as support for the communitarian model, she attempts to bolster that case by warning against the dangers posed by other religious voices in the public sphere:

> [W]e are [presently] confronted by those who claim to speak in the name of faith, but who offer a different version of what God expects of us; those who proclaim themselves the upholders of family values yet who do not value individual rights or personal autonomy, and who have little respect for the Constitutional principles that have allowed religion to thrive in this country unfettered by government coercion or corruption.... If we don't bring [our] progressive *religious* values [emphasis added] into the public arena with us, we will abandon the public square to those offering a different view of religion and values.[33]

In short, Feldman presents a twofold case for communitarian advocacy by the Reform Movement: (1) religious groups have a positive right—and the Reform Movement a prophetic mandate—to bring their particular conceptions of the good into the public square, and doing so has often produced positive results; and (2) if the Reform Movement refrains from bringing its progressive religious views into the public arena, it will cede that ground to other religious groups that are already there and that advocate values that are anathema to Reform Judaism.

It is in relation to such groups that the Movement demonstrates, on the other hand, an anti-communitarian disposition. For example, in a 2005 press release applauding a court ruling against supporters of teaching intelligent design in public schools, RAC Director Rabbi David Saperstein asserts that

> The scientific theory of evolution is being challenged in public schools and in our courts by *those seeking to tear down the wall of*

separation between church and state by enshrining *one religious view* [emphases added] into public school curricula. This campaign is dangerous, especially to those who cherish true religious liberty.... Objective scientific processes and theories must never be subverted to serve religious, political or ideological goals... As Jewish Americans, members of a religious minority, we understand, as did the framers of our Constitution, that our government must serve Americans of all faiths and no faith.[34]

Saperstein's critique of intelligent-design proponents as wrongly seeking to enshrine "one religious view" in government policy is noteworthy, particularly in light of the URJ Iraq war resolution, which advocates that the U.S. government make policy decisions regarding the war in accordance with one particular view of Jewish tradition. Does the URJ resolution similarly "[seek] to tear down the wall of separation between church and state" and endanger "those who cherish religious liberty"?

The RAC also condemns those who favor a Constitutional amendment banning same-sex marriage, stating in a press release that

> In a country created to protect the rights of all people, it is tragic that those who advocate on behalf of this amendment would codify in the Constitution *the religious teachings of some* [emphasis added] rather than protect the freedoms of all.[35]

Likewise, a letter to members of Congress, authored by the RAC and signed by a number of religious organizations, argues against the Federal Marriage Amendment in part because "It is surely not the federal government's role to prefer one religious definition of marriage over another, much less to codify such a preference in the Constitution."[36] Again, these statements raise the question of why it is acceptable for the Reform Movement to advocate for Iraq war policies that are grounded in its religious views while, at the same time, it is illegitimate for others to advocate for a Constitutional amendment that embodies their religious views on same-sex marriage.

A liberal, anti-communitarian impulse is also evident in the Reform Movement even outside the context of confrontation with oppositional religious voices. For instance, in a washingtonpost.com column on the appropriate use of religious language in election campaigns, RAC Director Saperstein writes that

[I]n discussing policy, it is inappropriate to suggest that one should support or oppose a policy solely because of religious beliefs. Something that must be taken by faith alone does not allow itself to be tested in the free marketplace of ideas, a quality that is essential for democracy to work and for any kind of meaningful public policy debate to take place.[37]

Here, Saperstein argues for public discourse boundaries that are generally consistent with those articulated in Dworkin's integrated community model. While Saperstein does not exclude religious language from the public sphere entirely, he maintains that appropriate religious argumentation must adhere to certain guidelines. In this vein, he contends that it is improper to argue for a particular policy exclusively on the basis of a religious idea of the good, since neither that conception of the good nor the vocabulary in which the argument is articulated is accessible to all citizens. Perhaps this explains why the URJ Iraq resolution contains secular arguments for withdrawal in addition to its religious arguments. In any case, Saperstein's position here raises questions about the Movement's aforementioned professed belief in communitarian discourse and highlights the fractured nature of its outlook on the proper role of religious argumentation in the public sphere.

VI. Conclusion: Recommendations for Resolving the Tension

The URJ's 2007 Iraq War resolution demonstrates that, even as the Movement emphasizes religion-state separation as a primary value and concern, Reform leaders continue to engage in communitarian discourse by bringing their particular religious ideas of the good to bear on the secular American political community. The irony, of course, is that official Movement organs, rabbis, and lay Reform Jews alike frequently condemn others—particularly those on the Religious Right—for doing the same thing. While there are certainly good arguments for both the communitarian and integrated community models of discourse, it is not tenable for the Reform Movement to continue to engage in the former and, at the same time, maintain that others, particularly those with whom the Movement disagrees, must adhere to the latter. That is to say, it is not reasonable to argue that Reform Judaism has both the right and the prophetic duty to bring its values to the public square, yet insist that other religious groups that do the same are wrongly trying to impose a particular religious view on the rest of society.

The Reform Movement can remedy this tension by consistently aligning its advocacy methods with one of the two public discourse models discussed in this article. Both enable the Movement to continue to "bring [its] values into the public arena," but each provides its own distinct guidelines for doing so. In order to choose the one that best suits Reform Judaism's needs, we must carefully consider the potential salutary and adverse impacts of the use of religious argumentation in the public square by any group, including our own.

If we conclude that employing such argumentation in public discourse can lead to a harmful imposition of a particular religious view on all Americans and thus compromise religion-state separation, we ought to base our advocacy on Dworkin's integrated community model. This would require us to study Jewish teachings regarding a given policy issue in the private sphere—i.e., within our synagogues, organizations, and virtual community—where we share a common Jewish idea of the good. Once we have determined what Judaism teaches us about that issue, we would then articulate those values in the public sphere using the common vocabulary of the American political community. Upon entering the public arena, Jewish source citations and references to the demands of halachah would remain at home. We would thus continue to advocate for policies that reflect the Movement's values, but we would do so in terms that are accessible to, and subject to the scrutiny of, everyone in the public sphere.

Conversely, if we determine that bringing the particularistic teachings of our tradition into the public square enhances the quality, diversity, and overall health of American political discourse, we should not shy away from it. We should embrace Sandel's communitarian approach and affirm our place in the public arena alongside other religious groups who likewise believe that their particular traditions have something meaningful to contribute to the political debate. Doing so with integrity, however, would necessitate that we abandon the notion that arguing for public policies on the basis of particular religious teachings—whether Jewish, fundamentalist Christian, or any other tradition—represents a threat to American democracy and religion-state separation. We should instead welcome all ideas, secular and religious, into the public square for consideration and debate on their merits by all members of the political community.

This article has aimed to show that the mainstream Reform views that (1) the prophetic mandate necessitates bringing particularistic Jewish teachings to bear on public policy, and (2) that the separation of religion and state is jeopardized by religious argumentation because it seeks to impose one religious view on the whole of society, have created a noticeable tension in Reform advocacy and discourse in the public sphere. To answer the question posed in the opening paragraph: It does seem that, when we seek to uphold the one principle as we understand it, we necessarily violate the other. This tension is unsustainable because it casts a shadow on the integrity of Reform public advocacy. Perhaps this article will spark a needed discussion within the Reform community about how to resolve this "liberal dilemma."

Notes

1. URJ Executive Committee, "Resolution on the War in Iraq 2007," *Union for Reform Judaism Resolutions and Bylaws*, March 12, 2007, http://urj.org/_kd/Items/actions.cfm?action=Show&item_id=14211&destination=ShowItem, 4
2. See *Mishneh Torah*, Hilchot Melachim 5:1.
3. See Maimonides, *Sefer ha-Mitzvot, shoresh* 14: "It is known that war and the conquering of the cities cannot [occur] except with a king, the counsel of the Great Sanhedrin, and the High Priest.... Therefore public acts...that [relate to]...the Sanhedrin, prophet and king, or *milchemet reshut*...are not incumbent [upon us] except when the Temple stands." These three religious-political institutions are essential to the functioning of *hilchot milchamah* because, as J.D. Bleich notes, "War is sanctioned only when commanded by God, i.e., when divine wisdom dictates that such a course of action is necessary for the fulfillment of human destiny....[E]ven a *milhemet reshut* requires the acquiescence of the *urim ve-tumim*; the message transmitted via the breastplate of the High Priest is a form of revelation granting divine authority for an act of aggression." J.D. Bleich, "War and Non-Jews," in *Contemporary Halakhic Problems, Volume II* (New York: Ktav Publishing House, Inc., 1983), 160. Since only a king (or, in the post-monarchic period, the Sanhedrin) may instruct the High Priest to consult the *urim* and *tumim* (see BT Yoma 73b; Nachmanides, *Hosafot* to *Sefer ha-Mitzvot*, pos. comm. 17), the monarch and rabbinic council possess authority that no other political institution—Jewish or otherwise—can match. It is erroneous, therefore, to equate the U.S. president and Congress

with the Jewish king and Sanhedrin because the American institutions cannot inquire of God and, therefore, cannot obtain divine consent to wage war. Since *hilchot milchamah* require such divine authorization, the rubric cannot function in the absence of the king, Sanhedrin, and *urim* and *tumim*. For more on this, see Bleich's aforementioned article, as well as J.D. Bleich, "Preemptive War in Jewish Law," in *Contemporary Halakhic Problems, Volume III* (New York: Ktav Publishing House, Inc., 1989).

4. URJ Executive Committee, "Resolution on the War in Iraq 2007," 2–3.
5. Ibid., 2.
6. URJ Executive Committee, "Executive Committee Decision on Unilateral Action by the U.S. Against Iraq," *Union for Reform Judaism: By and About the Union President*, September 23, 2002, http://urj.org/about/union/leadership/yoffie/iraq/. In this document, the URJ leadership states that "The President should not act without Congressional approval of the use of force including any unilateral military action taken by the U.S." Though no textual sources are cited in that document, the 2007 resolution explains that "This model of cooperative decision-making [i.e., the requirement that the king obtain Sanhedrin consent for *milchemet hareshut*], balanced between the various branches of government, led the URJ in 2002 to support congressional efforts to require the President to come back to the Congress for approval before actually deploying troops." (URJ Executive Committee, "Resolution on the War in Iraq 2007," 3.)
7. URJ Executive Committee, "Resolution on the War in Iraq 2007," 3.
8. Ibid.
9. Ibid.
10. The resolution apparently cites the wrong *Mishneh Torah* paragraph, as *Melachim* 6:11 articulates the requirement to initiate war at least three days before Shabbat. While it is impossible to know for sure which paragraph the document means to cite, since the *Mishneh Torah* says no such thing about protecting innocent civilians, it is possible that it refers to *Melachim* 6:4, which specifies that "neither women nor children should be killed" in *milchemet hareshut*.
11. URJ Executive Committee, "Resolution on the War in Iraq 2007," 3.
12. Ibid., 1.
13. URJ, "Union for Reform Judaism Adopts Resolution on Iraq War; Opposes Escalation and Calls for Phased, Expeditious Withdrawal of Troops," *Union for Reform Judaism Press Room*, March 12, 2007, http://urj.org/about/union/pr/2007/iraq_resolution/.
14. URJ Executive Committee, "Resolution on the War in Iraq 2007," 9.

15. Ibid.
16. Indeed, this is the same problem faced by congregational rabbis whose credentials may be questioned should they endeavor to preach about the war from the pulpit.
17. Michael Sandel, "The Procedural Republic and the Unencumbered Self," in *Communitarianism and Individualism,* ed. S. Avineri and A. de-Shalit (New York: Oxford University Press, 1992), 18.
18. Ibid., 24.
19. Ronald Dworkin, "Liberal Community," in *Communitarianism and Individualism,* ed. S. Avineri and A. de-Shalit (New York: Oxford University Press, 1992), 206.
20. Ibid., 207.
21. Sandel, "The Procedural Republic," 14. He writes: "[D]espite its philosophical force, the claim for the priority of the right over the good ultimately fails. And…despite its philosophical failure, this liberal vision is the one by which we live."
22. Dworkin, "Liberal Community," 212–213.
23. URJ Executive Committee, "Resolution on the War in Iraq 2007," 5.
24. Ibid., 3.
25. Ibid.
26. Ibid.
27. Ibid., 4.
28. CCAR, "The Guiding Principles of Reform Judaism, 1937," *Platforms Adopted by the CCAR,* October 27, 2004, Section B, http://ccarnet.org/Articles/index.cfm?id=40&pge_prg_id=3032&pge_id=1656.
29. URJ, "Adopted Resolutions," *Union for Reform Judaism Adopted Resolutions,* http://urj.org/docs/reso/.
30. As quoted in Marla Feldman, "Why Advocacy Is Central to Reform Judaism," *Religious Action Center for Reform Judaism (RAC) Resources on the War in Iraq,* http://rac.org/_kd/Items/actions.cfm?action=Show&item_id=1655&destination=ShowItem.
31. Religious Action Center of Reform Judaism (RAC), "Church State Issues and the Reform Jewish Movement," *Religious Action Center Advocacy Resources,* http://rac.org/Articles/index.cfm?id=3321&pge_prg_id=11285&pge_id=2391.
32. Feldman, "Why Advocacy Is Central to Reform Judaism."
33. Ibid.
34. RAC, "Reform Jewish Leader Applauds Court Ruling in Intelligent Design Case," *Religious Action Center of Reform Judaism Press Room,* December 20, 2005, http://rac.org/Articles/index.cfm?id=1389&pge_prg_id=7037.
35. RAC, "Reform Jewish Leader Reacts to President's Endorsement of the Federal Marriage Amendment; Calls on Senate to

'Overwhelmingly Reject' Amendment," *Religious Action Center Press Room,* June 6, 2006, http://rac.org/Articles/index.cfm?id=1628&pge_prg_id=4506.
36. RAC, "Clergy Sign-On Letter Opposing the Federal Marriage Amendment," *Religious Action Center Advocacy Resources,* June 2, 2004, http://rac.org/advocacy/specialresources/archive/2004fma/.
37. David Saperstein, "Guidelines for Candidates to Avoid Abusing Religion," *On Faith,* washingtonpost.com, January 26, 2007, http://newsweek.washingtonpost.com/onfaith/david_saperstein/2007/01/guidelines_for_candidates_to_a.html.

Examples of Rabbinic Advocacy

Rabbis for Obama: The Role of Rabbinic Leadership in the 2008 Presidential Campaign

Samuel N. Gordon

In June 2008 Rabbi Steve Bob and I met with others at the Chicago Jewish Leadership Committee for Obama. At that time the polls were showing that Senator Obama had about 60 percent of the Jewish vote nationally. This was a very high percentage of support in comparison with almost all other ethnic groups, but we were told that, with the exception of Jimmy Carter, no recent Democratic candidate had won the presidency with less than 75 percent of the Jewish vote; John Kerry had gotten 74 percent.

Immediately following that meeting, Rabbi Steve Bob and I created Rabbis for Obama. This was an unprecedented effort to publicly support Barack Obama for president. This type of rabbinic action had never been done before in America. As rabbis we were very concerned about issues surrounding public endorsements, confusion of our roles as rabbis to our congregants, and the tax implications of rabbis favoring one candidate in a partisan election. We had always been careful not to use our rabbinic position for political purposes. But in this election we felt that our voices needed to be heard in response to the vicious lies and accusations that some were spreading in an attempt to portray Senator Obama as a dangerous "other." The Jewish community was being manipulated into thinking he would be bad for American Jews and for

---

SAMUEL N. GORDON (C80) is the founding rabbi of Congregation Sukkat Shalom of Wilmette, Illinois, and has an M.B.A. from Northwestern University's Kellogg Graduate School of Management. He co-founded Rabbis for Obama.

Israel. Many of these smears and innuendoes were specifically targeted to Jewish voters. We felt we had to respond, and we did so by creating Rabbis for Obama.

While we still did not endorse Senator Obama from the pulpit or support his candidacy through our congregations, as individual rabbis we knew that we could add credibility to his campaign and help answer those who were playing on potential fears within our community. These tactics had begun very early in the campaign. When Senator Obama first announced his candidacy, because I am from Chicago, I began to hear from colleagues from throughout the country asking about Senator Barack Obama. Some had heard rumors that he was raised and educated in an Islamic madrasa in Indonesia and was a secret Muslim. Soon stories were circulating about his association with his pastor, Reverend Jeremiah Wright of Chicago. These stories usually included references to Reverend Wright's admiration for Louis Farrakhan. Others wrote to me after hearing that Senator Obama's Middle East advisors were Zbigniew Brzezinski and Robert Malley.

This was not the Barack Obama I knew. The real Barack Obama had deep ties to the Chicago Jewish community. I knew his mentors, those who had helped shape his career and who were major influences on his ideas. Prominent and respected Jews such as Newton Minow and Abner Mikva were among his earliest supporters who encouraged him and guided him from the time he was a law student at Harvard University.

I remember especially the night I attended a dinner in Chicago for the organization, Facing History and Ourselves. The program included Senator Barack Obama speaking with students from two Chicago high schools. One of the young students posed this question: "Senator Obama, why did you decide to give up the benefits of a career in a corporate law firm on Wall Street and instead choose public service?" Senator Obama responded: "When I was at Harvard Law School I had a teacher who changed my life—Martha Minow." I happened to be sitting at the table with Martha Minow, her parents, my good friends Newton and Jo Minow, and Abner Mikva. All of us sat there in amazement and with great pride in Martha.

Martha Minow, as a law professor at Harvard, had told her father that the brightest, most talented law student she had ever had was a young man named Barack Obama. Martha's father, Newton

Minow, was managing partner at Sidley and Austin, a major Chicago law firm. Newton Minow is best known for his role as chairman of the Federal Communications Commission under President Kennedy, but in Chicago he is a man who connects people with each other. Newt Minow brought Barack Obama to Chicago to work at Sidley and began to introduce him around. Barack Obama soon got to know other major Chicago Jewish figures such as Abner Mikva, Lester Crown, and many others. From that time on, Barack Obama was deeply connected to the Chicago Jewish world. I also knew some of those whom he chose for advisors: Dennis Ross, Anthony Lake, Daniel Kurtzer, Robert Wexler, and Mel Levine helped shape his ideas about Israel and the Middle East.

In January the Obama campaign asked me to appear in a video talking about Senator Obama's faith and integrity. I told of being a guest at his Senate swearing-in ceremony when he took the oath of office on a family Bible held by his wife, Michelle. It was a bit odd testifying to his Christian faith when there was nothing wrong with the fact that Congressman Keith Ellison had, in fact, been sworn into office using Thomas Jefferson's Koran, but it was necessary to respond to the lies about Senator Obama. I concluded the video by quoting the Book of Proverbs, saying, "Where there is no vision, the people perish" (Prov. 29:18). I spoke of the fact that, to me, Barack Obama was a man of vision, integrity, faith, and character.

I continued to respond to those who questioned Senator Obama's patriotism, positions on Israel, and his relationship with the Jewish community, but once his nomination as the Democratic candidate was clear, it was all the more important that Jewish leaders unite to help him win the Jewish vote. Rabbis for Obama was formed for that purpose. This was a grassroots effort. While we were in touch with the Obama campaign, we did not receive funding or direction from them. Rabbi Steve Bob and I worked with volunteers to build a Web site and contact our colleagues. Through word of mouth and the various rabbinic listservs, we put out the word that Rabbis for Obama existed. We recruited key rabbinic colleagues who had credibility within the four major Jewish denominations. They became our vice chairs, who were then able to work with their own contacts to build our organization. By the end of the summer, Rabbis for Obama included over 570 rabbis who were publicly willing to support Barack Obama for president.

There were many other rabbis who expressed their support for Obama but were reluctant to publicly endorse him. We understood their hesitancy but knew that they shared our desire to see Senator Obama become president. We used Rabbis for Obama as a vehicle to answer the false charges against Senator Obama. We asked our members to respond to the smears in whatever way they could. We wanted to create viral responses to the viral e-mails. It was important, however, for us to make clear that we did not want our colleagues to use their congregational positions to endorse Senator Obama. We did ask them to urge their congregants to choose their favorite candidate based on truth and not on lies. We provided fact sheets and information to our members. We were able to include Rabbis for Obama on various conference calls run by the Jewish Leadership Council for Obama. We received invaluable help from Eric Lynn, Adam Weissmann, and Daniel Shapiro with the Obama campaign. The Jewish and secular press wrote reports about our group, and we felt that our organization demonstrated that there was a significant group of Jewish leaders who believed in Senator Obama and who rejected the lies being told about him.

Most importantly, there was the extraordinary conference call with Senator Obama to nine hundred rabbis a few days prior to Rosh HaShanah. Rabbi Steve Bob and I had been asking the Obama campaign to arrange a conference call for the rabbis with someone like Ambassador Dennis Ross or Congressman Robert Wexler. On Monday afternoon, September 15, we received a call from the campaign that told us that Senator Obama himself would be available for a conference call on Wednesday morning. We had less than two days to organize the call, but through our network we were able to publicize the call, and by Wednesday over nine hundred rabbis participated in the call.

Senator Obama spoke for almost thirty minutes and then took questions from the heads of the four major branches of American Judaism. Senator Obama was thoughtful, insightful, and sincere. He spoke of the daunting task ahead of him. He acknowledged that there would be limits to what he could do, but he comfortably quoted from *Pirkei Avot* and the words of Rabbi Tarfon:

> Repairing all of that is a task that is beyond any one man or one woman. It can be daunting and I do not presume that I can, as president, repair all of this on my own. I am absolutely convinced

that when we come together with determination we can make the situation better. I know that one of the most profound Jewish teachings is that you are not required to complete the task but neither are you free to desist from it. That, I think, is what we have to do: we have to begin the hard task of repairing our economy and our foreign policy and that is, in my mind, what this election is all about.

Perhaps his most moving statement referred to the High Holy Day *machzor* and the shofar service. He spoke of the prayer in the shofar service that says: "Arouse you slumberers from out of your sleep." He tied that to the idea that America had been slumbering these past eight years and that it was now up to us to rouse our country and awaken to the task ahead:

> I know that the shofar is going to be blown in your synagogues over Rosh HaShanah, and there are many interpretations of its significance. One that I have heard, that resonates with me, is rousing us from our slumber so that we recognize our responsibilities and repent for our misdeeds and set out on a better path. The people in every community across this land [who] join our campaign, I like to think that they are sounding that shofar to rouse this nation out of its slumber and to compel us to confront our challenges and ensure a better path. It's a call to action. So as this New Year dawns, I am optimistic about our ability to overcome the challenges we face and the opportunity that we can bring the change we need not only to our nation but also to the world.

Never before had so many of America's rabbis come together to hear a major presidential nominee reflect on his relationship with the Jewish community and share his vision for a better future. I had the privilege and honor of welcoming everyone to the call and introducing Senator Obama. Rabbi Elliot Dorff, vice-chair of the Conservative Movement's Committee on Jewish Law and Standards and professor at the American Jewish University in Los Angeles offered an opening text study. Following Senator Obama's remarks, leading rabbis from the four major denominations posed questions to the senator, including Rabbi Jeffrey Wohlberg of the Rabbinical Assembly of Conservative Judaism, Rabbi Tzvi Hersh Weinreb of the Orthodox Union, Rabbi Eric Yoffie of the Union of Reform Judaism, and Rabbi Dan Ehrenkrantz of the Reconstructionist Rabbinical College.

The rabbis were deeply impressed by Senator Obama's depth of knowledge and insight, though some of what he said could have been dismissed as talking points created by talented speech writers—but no writers prepared him for the questions. Our Orthodox colleague, Rabbi Weinreb, asked about Senator Obama's position on government support of parochial schools, an issue important to the Orthodox community. Senator Obama did not hesitate to offer an answer that was against the position of Rabbi Weinreb. He clearly stated that he was opposed to publicly funded vouchers for private and parochial schools. But then Senator Obama expanded the conversation and spoke of his own commitment to early childhood education, after-school enrichment programs, and summer school opportunities. He said that the public schools could not be expected to handle all those needs and that faith-based educational programs would deserve support so long as they did not discriminate. And then Senator Obama demonstrated his personal knowledge of the Jewish community. He said he knew well and admired the Orthodox day school established by the Crown family in Chicago. It was impressive that he was familiar with the Ida Crown Academy of Chicago, and he demonstrated that he did not need to be briefed ahead of time to know what was happening in the Jewish community he represented.

A few days after the phone call, I was fortunate enough to be with Senator Obama and had the chance to speak with him about his impressions of the phone call. He was delighted to learn of its success, and he was grateful for the opportunity to speak to such a large group of rabbis. He spoke to me of his deep respect for the role that religious leaders play in America, and he extended that respect to the rabbis of America. The Jewish and secular press gave us great coverage.

Around this time the Obama campaign released a video of Jewish leaders speaking about their own relationship with Senator Obama and their trust in and support of him. This video was widely circulated in the Jewish community, and it was an important addition to the efforts to add to his credibility among skeptical Jews. Among those interviewed were John Levi, a prominent Chicago attorney, son of former Attorney General Edward Levi and grandson of Rabbi Emil G. Hirsch of Chicago Sinai Congregation. Judge Abner Mikva spoke of his long association with the senator. Lee Rosenberg, a leader of AIPAC, spoke, as did Susan Hattis,

Representative Jeff Schoenberg, Penny Pritzker, and Lester Crown. I was the rabbinic presence and voice on that video.

As the election drew near, many people were recognizing the role that Rabbis for Obama had played in the campaign. *Haaretz* newspaper named Rabbi Steve Bob and me two of the thirty-six American Jews who had had the greatest impact on this presidential election. I was also receiving numerous personal calls from people throughout the country. The Saturday before the election I was at home and the phone rang. I saw from the caller ID that it was a North Carolina call and the name was unfamiliar. I answered the phone, and a woman with a deep southern accent asked if I was Rabbi Gordon. I told her I was. She then asked if I was the same Rabbi Gordon she found on a Barack Obama donor list. Once again, I said I was that same Rabbi Gordon. She then expressed surprise. I asked her why. "Well," she said, "You are a rabbi and you are supporting Barack Obama, and I was told that Senator Obama is bad for the Jews." I reassured her that Senator Obama was in fact good for the Jews and for Israel. She said: "I am a Christian woman, and I was always taught that we had to be good to the Jewish people because they are the people of the Old Testament, but I have been told that Senator Obama is not good for the Jews." "No ma'am," I said, "Senator Obama is a friend of the Jewish people, and I know him and I can assure you that he is a very good man."

She thanked me for my response and said that I had made her feel much better. She said that she had planned to vote for Senator Obama but had been worried about the rumors she was hearing. Now she felt comfortable voting for him. I thanked her, and that was the end of our conversation.

On Tuesday night, November 4, I was in Grant Park in Chicago for what we hoped would be a victory celebration. The evening was beautiful, an unseasonably warm November night. I arrived early and made my way to the front of the stage. I saw a few friends from the Jewish community, and we stood around in a very joyful but expectant mood. As time wore on, more and more people joined the crowd, but we remained standing in the front row. As Jewish activists, we were especially delighted that Obama had won Florida, Pennsylvania, Michigan, and Ohio. At 10 P.M. the polls closed and Barack Obama was immediately declared the winner. We rejoiced. It was a thrilling moment.

Not long afterwards, Senator John McCain delivered a gracious and generous concession speech. Barack Obama soon emerged on the stage with Michelle and their two daughters. He was smiling and joyous, but I saw his shoulders drop for a moment, and he took the podium in a serious, though upbeat mood. His speech was lyrical and inspiring, but it was a victory tempered by the realities of a nation in serious trouble. As he had in his conference call with the rabbis, he tempered his remarks with the recognition that he could not be expected to complete the task, not in one year or one term. He was sharing a vision of America with words that resonated with the phrases of Lincoln. He was freed of the burden of a very difficult and nasty campaign, but the work ahead would be daunting and challenging, and he asked for a country united in dedication to that task.

I remained in Grant Park until 1:30 A.M., and at the end of the evening, the president-elect and Michelle came to the tent where we were, and we had a last chance to shake hands and congratulate them both. It was a thrilling moment mixed with the exhaustion of a very long day. Within a day or two, the exit polling results were in. The Jewish vote was estimated at between 78 and 79 percent for Obama. That was extraordinary. Our work had paid off. There was no way to know the impact of Rabbis for Obama or of the thousands who made phone calls or went door to door or lobbied friends and family. Ed Koch, Michael Bloomberg, Alan Dershowitz, Edgar Bronfman, and so many others reassured skeptical Jewish voters of Obama's commitment to Jewish values. Sarah Silverman might have helped with her video promoting "The Great Schlep." But it may well be that Sarah Palin had the greatest impact on the Jewish vote. But whatever the cause, the Jewish vote was overwhelmingly pro Obama, and for many of us, there is a feeling of deep gratification.

Rabbis for Obama: A Rabbi for Obama

Steven Bob

Recently members of my congregation, Etz Chaim, have expressed surprise to see me, a Cubs fan, drinking coffee from a Sox mug. I explained that it was a gift from a bar mitzvah boy. He had seen all the Cubs items in my office. He told me, "I know you are a Cubs fan, but you have to be a rabbi to Sox fans also."

I understand that even though I am deeply committed to one political party, I have to be a rabbi to Democrats and to Republicans. I am very careful not to use any platform provided by the congregation, physical or virtual, to endorse candidates. I follow the rules of the IRS and build a fence around those rules through my own good judgment. But this does not mean that I have to withdraw totally from the American political process.

I know many people complain about politics. I enjoy politics. I read political history and I participate actively in the political process. I have been involved in politics since I was a little boy. I checked coats when my parents hosted a fund-raising event in our home for Walter Mondale as he ran for attorney general of Minnesota.

I have been involved in lots of elections, not as a rabbi, just as a citizen. In 1992 I was even on the ballot to be a delegate to the Democratic National Convention. In the 2008 Presidential election I became involved in electoral politics as a rabbi for the first time.

A convergence of factors called me to act as a rabbi. Two factors called me to become involved in this election in a serious way. And two additional factors called me to act as a rabbi.

I was appalled by eight years of Republican rule. As Seth Meyers said, "George Bush broke the world." The war in Iraq was a tragedy of judgment compounded by an arrogance of execution. Under

---

STEVEN M. BOB (C77), the senior rabbi of Congregation Etz Chaim in Lombard, Illinois, is the founder of the Fourth Day Initiative, an interfaith solar energy project.

Republican leadership the economy neared total collapse. The Bush administration disregarded the powerless in our society and attacked our civil liberties. It was clear to me as an American that our country could not afford another four years of a Republican presidency.

In contrast Barack Obama offered the hope of a new vision for America. In many presidential elections we have heard the public complain that neither candidate seems special. Obama clearly stood out as something different. He combined intelligence, clear thinking, and deep concern. His uplifting rhetoric spoke to our hearts and to our heads. He stood out as a person who could lead our country and the world.

As a rabbi, I noticed that both parties had become particularly interested in Jewish votes. The concentration of Jews in the key swing states of Florida, Pennsylvania, and Ohio drew the interest of both campaigns. Each party wished to convince the Jewish community to support its candidate, thinking that Jews could provide the winning margin for their side.

The Republican Jewish Coalition and other supporters of Senator McCain chose scare tactics in their play for Jewish votes. They relied upon guilt by association, slander, and lies to attempt to drive a wedge between Senator Obama and the Jews. The Republicans tried to tie Senator Obama to Louis Farrakhan and Jesse Jackson. They stated that Senator Obama was turning to well known anti-Israel figures such as Zbigniew Brzezinski.

As a Jewish leader I could not sit idly by while the other side spilled blood. If the other side had limited itself to honest criticism, to disagreement on policy, my participation in the campaign could have been as in past years, as a citizen. The Republican campaign strategy moved me to act as a rabbi.

Over the years I have read articles and participated in conversations about who are the true leaders of the American Jewish community. Many people have opinions as to what role should be played by rabbis, federation executives, business leaders, etc.

In truth, genuine leaders are those who lead rather than those who participate in symposiums on leadership. Who gave Theodor Herzl the authority to convene the first World Zionist Congress? Theodor Herzl!

At a synagogue in Boca Raton in May 2008, a man asked Senator Obama, "Who are your supporters in the Jewish community?" The Senator responded by describing his Jewish friends in Chicago.

Reading this report I thought it would have been a better response if Senator Obama could have said, "Here is a list of three hundred rabbis from across the country who have endorsed me for president."

I reached out to the Obama campaign with my idea for Rabbis for Obama. At the same time Rabbi Sam Gordon was having the same conversation about the need for Rabbis for Obama.

Rabbi Gordon and I began Rabbis for Obama with rabbis we knew. I wrote to my HUC classmates and other rabbis in Chicago. We then began reaching out to rabbis across the country. We asked rabbis who joined to recruit other rabbis in turn. They turned to their friends. We established connections across the country and across the streams. Technology provided the means for us to reach out to large numbers of rabbis. The ability to send e-mail allowed us to ask hundreds of rabbis to join. By Election Day we had a total of 580 Rabbis for Obama.

This was the first organization of its kind in American history. Never before had a large group of rabbis endorsed a presidential candidate. I consulted with Dr. Gary Zola of HUC, who in turn asked Jonathan Sarna of Brandeis. Neither of them could think of anything even remotely on this scale. The political moment, the technology, and our willingness to work combined to create this historic organization of rabbis.

The vast majority of the rabbis we asked said yes. They joined for the same reasons that had originally moved me. A couple of rabbis said no because they supported Senator McCain. Some rabbis said no because they believed there would be negative consequences for them if they said yes. They feared the anger of influential Republicans in their congregations. Some rabbis said no because they believed that rabbis should not endorse candidates. Some rabbis declined to join because they worked for national Jewish organizations.

Throughout summer 2008 we gathered members for Rabbis for Obama. Shortly after Labor Day 2008, we went public by launching a Web site and issuing a press release. Steve Rabinowitz of the Washington public relations firm Rabinowitz/Dorf provided pro bono support for our efforts. Through his efforts the *Forward*, *Haaretz*, and the JTA made use of the release. Many Jewish newspapers across the country combined the material in our press release and interviews with local members of Rabbis for Obama.

With the help of my son-in-law, Jason Howard, and other volunteers, we put together a serious Web page. The page displayed the ever-growing list of our members. It also contained brief articles that Jewish Obama supporters could use to counter the slanderous attacks on Senator Obama.

We did not ask the rabbis for money. In fact, Rabbis for Obama did not raise money or spend money. We asked rabbis for permission to use their names. We said to rabbis, "Trust us with your name." In essence we said to them, "You have spent your entire careers building a *shem tov*; put it in our hands."

The members of Rabbis for Obama reported very little difficulty with congregants. We maintained a high *m'chitzah* between Rabbis for Obama and our congregations. We did not use the name of synagogues in our lists. Rather we used names of cities and towns in which the rabbis lived. I did not use the support staff of my congregation. I handled all the office functions myself. I did not use the Constant Contact program of Etz Chaim. All of our e-mail came from my private e-mail address.

As Rabbis for Obama, we were not individual rabbis telling their congregants how to vote. It was us, as a group, saying to the American Jewish Community, "Voting for Obama is Kosher." We gave our collective *hechsher* to Senator Obama. Rabbis for Obama gave rabbis a means to be involved in the presidential campaign as rabbis but outside the context of their own congregations.

I did receive hate mail. Some of it was unsigned but many of my harshest critics signed their names. One critic wrote, "You people call yourselves Rabbis. I recommend that each one of you take a gun and shoot yourselves in the head and save us the misery of calling yourselves Jews." Another critic wrote, "In fact a better name for "Rabbis for Obama" would be "Rabbis for Hamas." Some critics used images from the Holocaust: "It's becoming increasingly easy to understand how so many Jews packed a bag and walked down to the train heading to Auschwitz." Another wrote, "My grandfather told me about Jews like you, Judenrats."

We also received fan mail. The morning after the election, Dan Shapiro, who led the Obama campaign's outreach to the Jewish community wrote to us:

Rabbi Bob and Rabbi Gordon—

There is no way we can thank you enough for all that you did in conceiving and bringing to life Rabbis for Obama. As you surely know, Barack took 78 percent of the Jewish vote yesterday, and we won every swing state with a major Jewish population that we targeted. You and your colleagues played a huge part in making that happen—you lent great credibility to everything we were trying to educate people about. So thank you for all your amazing work. Last night was one of the most incredible moments any of us will experience. We hope you take great pride and satisfaction in helping make it possible.

With much gratitude and respect,

Dan

The members of my congregation, both Republicans and Democrats, continue to see me as their rabbi. Recently an Etz Chaim member who is a Republican made a point of telling me that he appreciated that I had kept a clear separation between my work as rabbi of the congregation and my political activities.

On December 16, 2009, my wife, Tammie, and I attended a Chanukah party at the White House. This was my second visit to the White House. My first visit was as a fourteen-year-old tourist in 1964. In 1964, I could not have dreamed that I would return as a rabbi to the White House, where an African American President would preside over the lighting of Chanukah candles.

Standing in the White House looking at the Chanukah candles and the Obamas, I could not help thinking about my family. I thought about my grandparents and great-grandparents, who came to this country from Lithuania and worked in the needle trades as tailors and upholsterers.

I thought about the president's family and Michelle's family. I marveled at the country we have built, from sea to shining sea. I reflected on the powers and possibilities that democracy provides for us. I thought about how our words and our deeds can light the candles of hope.

Scariest Night

Jerrold Goldstein

We gathered in the courtyard of First Baptist Church in St. Augustine, Florida. The sun was just setting on a hot, humid evening. Leaders organized us for the short walk downtown. They had led walks like this every evening for the past couple of weeks, and most of our fellow walkers were local folks who knew the routine quite well.

The group of walkers included about 150 people—men, women, and children—most of them African Americans. This evening's walkers also included sixteen Reform rabbis. I was one of those rabbis.[1] The leader of our procession was the Reverend Martin Luther King Jr., president of the Southern Christian Leadership Conference. The date was June 17, 1964.

Now I am a generally optimistic and self-confident person. At age twenty-eight, I had already traveled in the United States and Europe and lived for a year in Israel. I saw nothing particularly difficult about a half-mile walk on paved streets in an American city. Our destination was also of historical interest. We were headed to a classic tourist site in St. Augustine, the Old Slave Market.

King gave us a little orientation talk. "Remember," he said, "We are committed to nonviolence. There may be some hecklers along the way downtown who will object to your presence on the streets. They may taunt you with insults and challenge your motives. Never let them lead you to question your own integrity. Above all, never let them provoke you to violent response! Do not even answer their insults. What we want is well known. We have learned well the lessons of democracy and of our Judeo-Christian tradition. We must protest vigorously when we are denied rights

---

JERROLD GOLDSTEIN (C63) volunteers as secretary of the pluralistic Sandra Caplan Community Bet Din of Southern California. Before professional retirement, he served as rabbi of congregations and Hillel units and then as a staff person of the Union for Reform Judaism.

guaranteed to us as citizens by the Constitution of the U.S. and which are ordained by God for all men, but we will not resort to violence."

That perspective sounded good to me. So I lined up as instructed. We were to walk side by side in pairs in one long line. City authorities had approved the parade route and opened the streets for our access. We would march right down the center line of the streets all the way to the Old Slave Market, where we would form a circle, sing a song, recite a prayer, and receive a blessing from King. Just to be on the safe side, the governor of Florida had dispatched a unit of state highway patrolmen to accompany us on our walk.

That plan sounded good to me—reassuring. The whole thing was well organized. Nothing to be afraid of. I was actually looking forward to this mini-tour of downtown St. Augustine.

So we headed off to our destination with confidence and eager anticipation. Out of the church courtyard and into the middle of the street, walking at a normal pace, we proceeded. The highway patrolmen were out there and they fell in at regular twenty-five-foot intervals to our left and right. One of my colleagues recalls that the little girl marching next to him "was squeezing my hand very tight."

The column swung out onto Main Street. I'll never forget the sight. On both sides of the street, crowds of silent spectators were standing and waiting for the show. Half the white people of St. Augustine had come to watch from the sidewalk. Like Romans at the ancient coliseum, the spectators were there to smell the blood. And we were the event!

Tough gladiators were standing on the curbs closest to us walkers. Hundreds of hostile people. These folks were noisy and really angry. They shouted ugly hateful insults at us. There were even parents with kids who joined in the jeering:

"You're a bunch of Communists!"
"This is our city!"
"Go back where you came from!"
"We don't need you nigger-lovers!"

Even more menacing were the red-faced rednecks who stood on the street corners with baseball bats, broken bottles, and bricks in their hands. Never in my life had I ever confronted such raw hostility focused on me. It was clear to me that these hoodlums would love to throw the glass pieces and jagged stones at us walkers.

We walked straight ahead, but I was totally aware that a serious threat was just fifteen feet to my left or right. A thin line of twenty uniformed highway officers protected us from the violent attack. But the patrol men let us know that they were not happy to walk with us. They were themselves men of the white South and they had a job tonight that was quite unpleasant for them. They were assigned to keep the peace by protecting a band of black and Jewish agitators who had come to north Florida with no appreciation for the wholesome traditions of a southern community.

Walking that half-mile gauntlet to the Old Slave Market downtown and then back again to the Baptist Church was the most frightening experience of my whole life. I knew then that if chaos broke out I would be bloodied, maybe even killed. That was the night when I learned the meaning of courage. I had put myself in a highly dangerous situation, and it could have become a fatal choice. I was lucky that the state troopers provided a thin line of protection. Violence did not occur that night, but it did happen in St. Augustine and other places on many other days during that season.

What I want to write about here is why I went to St. Augustine, what I think was accomplished in 1964, and how the support of Mount Zion Temple mattered to me.

I was a young rabbi then who had come to St. Paul with his wife directly from ordination at the Hebrew Union College in Cincinnati. A note in the Mount Zion Bulletin a couple of years ago stated that 150 current Temple families were members 40 years ago. Some of these old timers surely remember how shocking it was when their young rabbi was arrested in St. Augustine and charged with three criminal counts: trespassing with malicious intent, breach of peace, and conspiracy. The St. Paul *Pioneer Press* reported that Mount Zion's Rabbi Goldstein was "arrested with great violence" and then sent to St. John County Jail. Mount Zion Temple was and is a respectable old synagogue with a dignified tradition. Clergy from houses of worship like this do not commit crimes and go to jail!

I have clippings of old newspaper articles reporting the details of my arrest and jail time. Newspaper articles always focus on details

SCARIEST NIGHT

of arrest and the jail time. Nothing was written about the scary Wednesday night walk. The Thursday arrest got all the media attention. If the thugs had beaten me up, then that might have been the story. But the press was unable to convey the deep significance of the walk. Sixteen white rabbis from all over the country had joined the African American struggle for equal rights in a Florida city—and the media focused it simply as an outrageous arrest and jailing of rabbis.

I was actually arrested because I invited a black man to be my guest for lunch. He and I were going to enter a nice St. Augustine restaurant, sit down, and order our meals like two respectable gentlemen. That was the "conspiracy" with which I was charged.

Of course I knew in 1964 that all decent restaurants and public facilities in St. Augustine were segregated by city law, open only to white people. Nevertheless, tourists from every state in the Union were enthusiastically invited to visit the city and enjoy its hospitality. Tourism was the basis of the city's commerce, and in 1964 St. Augustine touted its four hundredth anniversary as "oldest city in the United States." It promoted itself as an American historical shrine and a notable place to visit. I was a white man from Minnesota and I was a welcome visitor. But my black friend from Alabama was not welcome. This legalized exclusion of all nonwhite Americans from public facilities in St. Augustine seemed to us like a major violation of the federal laws on interstate commerce. I knew that the police would not let my friend and me sit together and order lunch in any restaurant, but we wanted to create the grounds for a court case challenging the municipal segregation ordinances.

In fact, the city police never even let us get into the Chimes Restaurant. They arrested us immediately after we parked our car in the restaurant's lot. We had wanted to stand in a small prayer circle before we entered the restaurant and the adjoining motel, and the police called that "conspiracy, "disturbing the peace," and "trespassing with malicious intent." We were actually reciting the Psalm 23 when arrested.[2]

My Yom Kippur sermon three months later in 1964 was one of the best that I ever gave. I spoke about the reasons for my participation in the St. Augustine events. I called my sermon "The Sin of Silence" and I talked about the sin of inaction when we behold calculated acts of injustice. How often it happens that we are able to see something wrong going on, but we just stand by without getting involved. We don't want to get hurt or to make fools of ourselves. So we just become spectators of the passing parade, excusing ourselves from an opportunity to make a moral difference.

Rabbi Harold Schulweis of Los Angeles writes of the "inextricable bond" between belief and behavior in Judaism. "Faith," he teaches, "is demonstrated not with the declarations of my mouth but with arms and legs." A recitation of creed is not a demonstration of Jewish faith. Commitment to Judaism is demonstrated by what we do with our arms and legs—our bodies. To march with MLK was to put my body on the line with abused Americans of a key southern city. Some would say that this was political action, but I say that it was an act of spiritual sensitivity.

In June 1964, African Americans of St. Augustine stated their goals in three clear demands with which I, as a Jew, concurred:

1. Desegregation of all hotel and restaurant facilities;
2. Employment of qualified Negroes as firemen and policemen;
3. Establishment of a permanent biracial committee to deal with continuing problems.

Sadly, the town's whites totally ignored these requests. White St. Augustine leaders would never meet with blacks to discuss their goals. No newspaper would print their letters. No radio station interviewed black representatives. No local white clergy sided with the oppressed. So the blacks began a series of nonviolent demonstrations designed to attract attention to their grievances. And the white folks still neither said nor did anything about the injustice. They stood on the sidewalk and watched.

On the basis of my religious faith I believe that doing nothing is wrong. I am not allowed to stand on the sidewalk and watch. It is the sin of silence. I was not comfortable being part of the silent majority even though I was safely in Minnesota. When Martin Luther King called on American Rabbis to join him in St. Augustine, I was ready to get involved. I said "yes." I volunteered to demonstrate with my arms and legs the strength of my Jewish beliefs.

From our cell in the St. John County Jail, we sixteen rabbis and the director of UAHC's Commission on Social Action made a joint statement on why we had come to St. Augustine. Here are three of its paragraphs:

We came because we could not stand silently by our brother's blood. We have been vocal in our exhortation of others, but the idleness of our hands too often revealed an inner silence. Silence has become the unpardonable sin of our time.

We came as Jews who remember the millions of faceless people who stood quietly, watching the smoke rise from Hitler's crematoria.

We came because we know that, second only to silence, the greatest danger to humans is loss of faith in our capacity to act.[3]

I believe that Judaism never separates faith from action. Jews have never given up our faith that the world can be a better place. If we want a just world, then we must do something more than pray for peace and justice. We must act like partners of God to bring more kindness, caring, and justice into the world. That's our kind of religion.

Almost from its founding 150 years ago, Mount Zion Temple has been a member of the Reform Movement, and a line of sincere rabbis has taught the congregation that Judaism stands for justice. This congregation may have been shocked by my arrest in St. Augustine, but it was not ashamed. Members came to me as soon as I returned to St. Paul and they individually volunteered to reimburse the bail charges for my release from jail. Many phoned or wrote with words of supportive appreciation. Never did the temple officers or board censure what I had done. The temple attitude was one of complete encouragement. They recognized my behavior as consistent with their synagogue's kind of religion.

A congregant, Ronna Paymar, wrote a note to me after my Yom Kippur sermon. Ms. Paymar's appreciation of my message validated my vision of a meaningful rabbinate and I've kept her fan letter for forty-five years as a continuing professional challenge.

Dear Rabbi Goldstein,

Unaccustomed as I am to writing "fan" letters, I feel I have to let you know how much I enjoyed your Yom Kippur day sermon. Even after the reams written, and thousands of words spoken on the racial issues before us today, you brought a fresh new voice that was a challenge to all of us. By your stand and actions this summer, I, as a Temple member take great pride in the fact that what you did somehow makes up for what I felt but couldn't do; and for that, I thank you.

During the summer months right after my arrest, the U.S. Congress passed the first of three great Civil Rights Acts. Those laws mandated an end to racial segregation in public hotels and restaurants. Finally, Congress had acted under federal interstate commerce powers to integrate all public facilities. That was a great victory for MLK and for America. I feel certain that we sixteen rabbis who marched in St. Augustine and went to jail enabled a clear step forward for justice in our country.[4]

Joshua Sobol, an Israeli playwright, has written a stunning drama called *iWitness* about the decision of an Austrian man in 1943 to refuse service in the German army. For making that decision, Franz Jagerstatter was executed by the Nazi military command. He is surely one of the great conscientious objectors of history, like Antigone and Mahatma Gandhi. I was greatly moved by Sobol's play when I saw it in English translation in a Los Angeles production. Few of us will ever come close to the great models of heroic moral decision. Still, the lives of those moral giants are a challenge to all of us. What is our life all about? For what do we live? How do we use our lives to make a difference?

I like this poem by C. P. Cavafy that I found in the program booklet of *iWitness*:

> To certain people there comes a day
> When they must say the great Yes or the great No.
> He who has the Yes ready within him
> Reveals himself at once, and saying it he crosses over
> To the path of honor and his own conviction.
> He who refuses does not repent. Should he be asked again,
> He would say No again. And yet that No—
> The right No—crushes him for the rest of his life.

In a sense, I was fortunate. I was able to engage myself in an historic civil rights breakthrough for the American people. Racial integration was a logical consequence of our democratic and Jewish principles, and a great "Yes" to that moment seems obvious in retrospect, although it was complicated at the time. But the moment has passed for Freedom Marches. No one reading this article can go back to 1964. Now the world has new issues, some of them very recognizable and some of them not yet visible: How can we remove lingering traces of racism from our nation? What shall be done about the inequities in education? How shall we have really fair elections? What are the limits of freedom in a multicultural society? How shall we protect our environment? How shall we organize the health care delivery system in a mature democracy? I don't know the right way to deal with each of these issues, but surely they will not go away by themselves. I trust that a path forward will be projected by some heir to Martin Luther King's legacy, and a new generation will have its own opportunity to declare a great "Yes" to the challenge. I pray that our nation is ready to take the required steps and that Jews of faithful conscience will lead the way.

One man who was a teenager at Mount Zion Temple when I went to St. Augustine is now a representative in the Minnesota State Legislature. He has made the "great Yes" a guiding principle of his politics. Whenever asked by journalists or constituents why he is such a strong advocate for social justice legislation, he always answers: "Because my rabbi was arrested in 1964." That is his symbolic way to declare a spiritual embrace of the social justice tradition in Judaism.

Notes

1. The sixteen rabbis were: Eugene Borowitz, Balfour Brickner, Israel Dresner, Daniel Fogel, Jerrold Goldstein, Joel Goor, Joseph Herzog, Norman Hirsh, Leon Jick, Richard Levy, Eugene Lipman, Michael Robinson, B. T. Rubenstein, Murray Saltzman, Allen Secher, and Clyde T. Sills. Albert Vorspan, then Director of the UAHC Commission on Social Action, was also present.
2. Wikipedia declares that this was "the largest mass arrest of rabbis in American history." Wikipedia, s.v. "St. Augustine Movement," http://en.wikipedia.org/wiki/St._Augustine_Movement.
3. From "Why We Went: A Joint Letter from the Rabbis Arrested in St. Augustine," a four-page brochure composed by the sixteen rabbis and Albert Vorspan during their night of imprisonment in St. John County Jail. It is available at the American Jewish Archives, Cincinnati.
4. Taylor Branch, *Pillar of Fire: America in the King Years, 1963–65* (New York: Simon & Schuster, 1998), 335–56, has an account of the events in St. Augustine as a part of what Branch calls "Freedom Summer." A week before our arrest, Martin Luther King had written from St. Augustine to Rabbi Dresner: "I would imagine that some 30 or so rabbis would make a tremendous impact on this community and the nation. We would hope that some would be prepared to submit to arrest." Ibid., 340.

It Wasn't a Giant Leap but a Natural Next Step

Allen I. Freehling

This CCAR symposium, which is focusing on the subject of "Politics and Spirituality," is of particular interest to me not only because of the direction that my rabbinic career has taken since 2002 but also because it has prompted me to reflect on the many ways in which my own spirituality has been enhanced when I have confronted the reality of politics and experienced the noble efforts of elected officeholders who have displayed all of the laudable attributes not of "politicians" but of "public servants."

Perhaps it would be helpful if I were to share with you some background information regarding my life's journey that has been unfolding during almost eight decades.

Rubbing Up against Prejudice

While the Freehling family has been in residence in Chicago since the mid-1800s, my own branch left there in 1938 to settle in Miami, where my parents, sister, and I encountered racism ("whites" and "coloreds" were constantly and hideously reminded that society intended to keep them separate and unequal), anti-Semitism (signs outside certain Miami Beach hotels proclaimed: "No Dogs, Cats, Negroes, or Jews Allowed"), a flowering American Nazi campaign (men and women emulating their counterparts in Germany challenged the soul of our nation's democracy in assembly halls and on city streets), and other forms of prejudice.

ALLEN I. FREEHLING (C67) is an alumnus the University of Miami, who spent ten years as an industrial and institutional administrator before entering HUC-JIR. After being ordained, he served as associate rabbi in Toledo and then became senior rabbi at University Synagogue in Los Angeles. Three decades later, he moved on to City Hall, where he managed the Human Relations Commission for seven years before becoming deputy chief of staff for a member of the City Council last July.

While my mom and dad were certainly not ritually observant Jews, they were active members of the community's largest Reform congregation (Temple Israel), which proved to be a cauldron for "social justice" where the teachings of our biblical prophets were constantly referred to by the synagogue's rabbis, who urged their congregants to be broadly and deeply involved in any and all struggles against discrimination and hate regardless of who was being targeted.

The vicissitudes of World War II were ever-present reminders of the fragile nature of liberty and how it must be nurtured and preserved—not just for some people but for all peoples. Within this context, adherents of Reform Judaism maintained a universalistic, inclusive point of view, which was certainly at odds with the turn toward particularism acted out by an increasing number of Orthodox Jews. Subsequently, against the backdrop of the Holocaust, the effort to give birth to Israel and to keep it viable convinced them that they could trust no one but themselves!

The Roots and Flowering of *Tikkun Olam*

In contrast with that turning inward and away from the community at large, throughout my childhood, adolescence, and early adulthood, I became more and more aware of the places within the fabric of our society that were tattered and in need of repair—though the concept of *tikkun olam* had not yet been employed to describe them. I had been taught that improvement and progress could only occur when we not only satisfied the urgings of our own self-interest but when we also established and maintained coalitions with others whose basic needs were not all that different from ours. So it seemed only natural that I should be engaged in both Jewish and non-Jewish activities that were of benefit to the whole of society.

A coalescence of skills and opportunities made this entry into public life seamless; early on, I volunteered to take on leadership roles, which led to many others being handed to me. Meanwhile, from the time I first embarked on an avocational career in radio broadcasting and writing while I was still a junior high school student, an escalating community profile permitted me to interact with an increasing number of decision-makers in both the public and the private sector.

As a result, my own spirituality was being developed as I worked with all kinds of people deeply involved in politics. We concentrated on identifying conditions that were adversely affecting certain sectors of our society and trying out problem-solving techniques designed to bring endangered children and adults out of their morass.

Career Choices and a Growing Awareness That God Is Always Nearby

Unlike most Reform rabbis, who walked a straight path from public school through a university and on to HUC-JIR, I did not turn to the rabbinate as an ultimate career until I reached the age of thirty, though I had been keenly aware of a gnawing compulsion toward this path since I was a young teenager. The community activism and work-related experiences of my first ten years out of college were really a training ground that eventually left me no choice but the rabbinic path.

Meanwhile, I had opportunities to go through a process of maturation in the midst of the fields of business and commerce (as a presidential assistant to a furniture manufacturer, a supermarket corporate head, and a public relations practitioner), higher education (as the assistant to a university president), and synagogue management (as the executive director of both a Reform and a Conservative congregation).

Lessons learned there were personally enriching and they were a strong influence on me as I shaped, molded, and implemented everything that I attempted to accomplish as a congregational rabbi and simultaneously as a Jewish and general community leader during the thirty-five years after I was ordained.

This involvement has fallen into certain categories, within the Jewish community and beyond it, in support of (1) enhancing government policy reform, (2) advancing health and human services, (3) making education more responsive to community needs, (4) advancing the cause of intergroup relations, and (5) enhancing the efforts of nongovernmental agencies. In every instance, Judaism's moral imperatives have been both the basis upon which I have acted and the driving force demanding that I remain focused on responding to the needs of a myriad of Jews and non-Jews who have been underserved and/or ignored altogether.

IT WASN'T A GIANT LEAP BUT A NATURAL NEXT STEP

A Move from the Synagogue to City Hall

At the conclusion of my serving for three decades as the senior rabbi at University Synagogue, the elected leadership determined that it was time for me to become the congregation's first rabbi emeritus. Thereafter, I incorporated a nonprofit organization that would concentrate on helping to resolve social justice issues; simultaneously, I registered précis for four books at the Writers' Guild, and several not-for-profit agencies weighed the possibility of my becoming a president/CEO.

However, what trumped all that post-congregational exploration was my appointment by the mayor of Los Angeles as the executive director of the city's Human Relations Commission. This assignment lasted for seven years, until a deplorable economic crisis caused problem-solvers to eliminate the HRC. On the heels of that very troublesome decision, a member of the City Council appointed me his deputy chief of staff.

An Imaginary Conversation

I have proffered this autobiographical sketch in order to set the stage for my writing about what I perceive to be the intersection of spirituality and politics. Let's embark on an imaginary conversation based on questions that you might ask and the answers I would give:

What are some of the expectations that are embedded in an officeholder's inviting a rabbi to serve on a public board/committee/commission?

In all likelihood, that public official has interacted with the rabbi in one or more arenas and has found this person to possess the ability to be both a secret-keeper and a truth-teller who objectively evaluates circumstances and candidly recommends long-lasting solutions against the backdrop of both historical perspectives and contemporary realities.

How is the rabbi treated by his non-clergy peers, who have also been appointed to serve in this capacity?

In most instances, while I always introduce myself as "Allen," almost always I am referred to—with deference and respect—as "the rabbi." This has been the experience I had when leading a congregation and it's one that has become familiar when I have invested time and energy in rendering volunteer assistance in both public and private sectors. For a variety of reasons, people seem to feel more comfortable addressing clergypersons by their titles rather than their first names. By the way, once I assumed full-time responsibilities in City Hall and began to cultivate collaborative partnerships and friendships, a considerable number of non-Jewish elected officials, department heads, and others have introduced me as "my rabbi."

Even though such service is acted out in the public arena and affected by political realities, is the rabbi able to remain focused on moral imperatives and bring them to the attention of those for whom and with whom she or he is working?

Absolutely! I am convinced that if an ordained person were appointed to assume the role of volunteer or professional leader in government, and that person failed to offer criticism, insights, and strategies rooted in religious principles, his or her value would quickly diminish and that would result in dismissal.

Are you always conscious of acting as a rabbi when carrying out your duties in City Hall?

When I exchanged my synagogue responsibilities for those in municipal government, the transition was seamless, because many of the people with whom I began to interact were men and women who had been allies in battles for social justice that we had waged during all the years I was a community activist. Also, much of my workload focuses on actualizing the demands of our biblical prophets, who insisted that all of us do everything we can to uphold the rights and champion the cause of those children and adults whom society all too often abandons, ignores, and dehumanizes. Those demands—articulated by our Sages—are timeless; they are at the heart of what city government does best when it is in sync with those constituents whose lives are often at risk as a result of their being culturally, economically, and socially deprived by individuals and groups who are filled with hate and who are biased, prejudiced, and quick to discriminate and to treat others with disdain. Often from the bimah we chastise those who do not love their neighbors as they love themselves; when serving in government, we are able not only to speak out in opposition to that kind of maltreatment, but to act in ways that can effectively lift up the downtrodden while neutralizing the efforts of their adversaries.

Finally, is it appropriate for rabbis to serve outside the Jewish community? How are you being a rabbi if you are occupying a civic position?

As far as I'm concerned, it's not only appropriate but it is essential that some of us venture outside our comfort zones, serve in other capacities, and thereby expand the very nature of our vocations. We rabbis have much to contribute to the world around us—it is a world that not only needs a strong and vibrant Jewish community but is enhanced by the influence of Judaism as embodied by those rabbis who choose to walk down different paths and to interact with non-Jews who wish to work with us, to learn from us and to teach us, and to be involved in making *tikkun olam* not just a viable parochial concept but a global reality in which politics—public service—is enriched and emboldened by our own awareness of spirituality that is manifest in so much of what we say and do in the community at large.

When Congregations Take Positions
The Jewish Case for Community Organizing

Power Precedes Program: Relationships and Politics in the Pulpit

Larry Bach

The Rev. William Sloane Coffin Jr. was known to tell this story: The pastor of a conservative congregation was about to be dismissed for his outspoken, liberal politics. His position was preserved, however, in a close vote of the board. Among those voting to keep him was a very politically conservative trustee. Why did this man vote to retain the pastor whose politics infuriated him so? "He held my wife's hand for the last day of her life, and for the next day, he held mine."[1]

Clergy sometimes tell this story, or a variation on it, to illustrate the value of tending to the pastoral side of our calling. Our political activities will be tolerated, we tell ourselves, as long as we are present for people in times of personal or familial need. In this narrative, tending to the personal relationships may be set in opposition to politics, with the roles of pastor and preacher in tension. In its most callous version of this narrative, pastoral work is something we *have to do* in order to provide needed cover for our public, political work. But there is another way of reading Coffin's anecdote: as a tale about the value and place of relational power.[2]

LARRY BACH (C98) is rabbi of Temple Mount Sinai in El Paso, Texas. He is a founder and past chairperson of Border Interfaith, a congregation-based community organization affiliated with the Industrial Areas Foundation.

This less utilitarian approach rejects the bifurcation of pastor and preacher roles and instead sees the building of relationships within our congregations as a pastoral *and* political activity. The lesson of Coffin's pastor is not that relationships must be built *so that* we'll have the opportunity to do justice; rather, the relationships are an *essential component* of our justice work and must in fact precede it.

That they precede it is the main point of this article. Had the pastor in Coffin's story not built the relationship *first,* he might have been let go in a close vote. Because he'd tended to the relationship, he stayed on in a close vote and was able to maintain the struggle. In community organizing parlance: power precedes program.

Power Precedes Program is a foundational teaching in the organizing tradition pioneered by Saul Alinsky and carried on today by training networks such as the Industrial Areas Foundation, DART (the Direct Action and Research Training Center), PICO (People Improving Community Organizing), and the Gamaliel Foundation. In one recent popular introduction to community organizing, the principle is described in these terms:

> Power is rarely built through a program. It is built through intentional relationships that knit together the fabric of a community—an organization. And once that organization is sufficiently built, *then* that organization can address issues and concerns of the people in significant ways, because it has the power to do so.[3]

A word about "power" is in order. Power has a bad reputation, owing to its abuse by political and religious figures down the ages. Lord Acton's famous dictum, "Power tends to corrupt, and absolute power corrupts absolutely,"[4] is often quoted by those who wish that religious institutions would stay focused on the spiritual and leave the bruising real world alone. But power is a neutral force. It is simply "the ability to act," in Hebrew, *y'cholet.* We find reference to power in this sense when Caleb countered the assessment of the spies: *yachol nuchal lah,* "we can overcome it" (Num. 13:30). If we accept the premise that one way to build that capacity is through building relationships, then we will find it no coincidence that two politically-oriented civil rights movements, both forged through the community-organizing model of relational power, are known by mottos that resonate with Caleb's words: "We shall overcome." "Sí, se puede." *Yachol nuchal.*[5]

Rabbis looking to "go public" in their pulpits will do well to remember that relational power is essential to their work. Reminders of this lesson can be found in our own textual tradition no less than in contemporary writing about community organizing (or stories about pastors nearly losing their jobs). A teaching of Yehudah Aryeh Leib Alter of Ger (1847–1905) can be read to make the case for relational power preceding, and enabling, action.[6]

The teaching is found in Alter's posthumously published Torah commentary, *Sefat Emet*.[7] It is a teaching on the opening verses of *Parashat Vayak'heil*, Exodus 35:1–20:

> [1] Moses then convoked the whole Israelite community and said to them:
> These are the things that the Lord has commanded you to do: [2] On six days work may be done, but on the seventh day you shall have a sabbath of complete rest, holy to the Lord; whoever does any work on it shall be put to death. [3] You shall kindle no fire throughout your settlements on the sabbath day.
> [4] Moses said further to the whole community of Israelites:
> This is what the Lord has commanded: [5] Take from among you gifts to the Lord; everyone whose heart so moves him shall bring them — gifts for the Lord: gold, silver, and copper; [6] blue, purple, and crimson yarns, fine linen, and goats' hair; [7] tanned ram skins, dolphin skins, and acacia wood; [8] oil for lighting, spices for the anointing oil and for the aromatic incense; [9] lapis lazuli and other stones for setting, for the ephod and the breastpiece.
> [10] And let all among you who are skilled come and make all that the Lord has commanded: [11] the Tabernacle, its tent and its covering, its clasps and its planks, its bars, its posts, and its sockets; [12] the ark and its poles, the cover, and the curtain for the screen; [13] the table, and its poles and all its utensils; and the bread of display; [14] the lampstand for lighting, its furnishings and its lamps, and the oil for lighting; [15] the altar of incense and its poles; the anointing oil and the aromatic incense; and the entrance screen for the entrance of the Tabernacle; [16] the altar of burnt offering, its copper grating, its poles, and all its furnishings; the laver and its stand; [17] the hangings of the enclosure, its posts and its sockets, and the screen for the gate of the court; [18] the pegs for the Tabernacle, the pegs for the enclosure, and their cords; [19] the service vestments for officiating in the sanctuary, the sacral vestments of Aaron the priest and the vestments of his sons for priestly service.
> [20] So the whole community of the Israelites left Moses' presence.

Below is the passage from the *Sefat Emet:*

> "So Moshe convoked the people..." (Exod 35:1a)..."These are the matters which God has commanded, to do..." (35:1b)..."Six days shall you work..." (35:2ff). This (material) preceded the account of the Tabernacle since the actual building the Tabernacle could happen only through the strength of that convocation (*bekoach hakehilah*). Thus it is said, "and I will dwell within them." As the midrash has it, "'Within it' is not written, but rather 'within them.'" See Alshich on Parashat Terumah. Now this convocation dealt with the Sabbath. To speak to them about the Sabbath—for this he convened them. And the verse "These are the matters..." refers to convocation as well. God commanded that they should create a community themselves (*sheyakhilu atzmam*). And all of this is one matter: the elevation of the whole Jewish people, which leads to the arrival of the Divine Presence, which is what the Sages call "*K'nesset Yisrael.*"
>
> "Six days shall you work..." The four winds, and up and down, representing the gathering of all of the forces, all aspects [of divinity], gathered to an inner point (*heichal linekudah hapenimit*)—namely, the Sabbath. This is the real "building of the Tabernacle," as it is written: "What house shall you build for me?..." (Is 66:1).

Speaking to his Chasidim on a Sabbath in March 1876,[8] Alter first observes that the commandment to keep the Sabbath (Exod. 35:2–3) preceded the commandment to build the Tabernacle (35:10–19), and that both were preceded by Moses' convoking of the people (35:1a, "Then Moses convoked the people..."). Applying the principle of *s'michut parshiyot*—the juxtaposition of proximate biblical passages—to draw out meaning, he concludes that "the building of the Tabernacle occurs through the strength of the community (*m'lechet haMishkan hu b'ko-ach hak'hilah*)." Thus three textual moments—the "convocation" of the people, which gives the *parashah* its name; the restatement of the prohibition against Sabbath labor; and the command to begin the work—are understood, each in light of the others.

The Hebrew-literate reader cannot fail to recognize in the verb *vayak'heil* the connection to *k'hilah*, "community." While our translation rightly has "convoked," conveying the plain-sense meaning of the people being gathered to a particular time and place to listen to Moses, we recognize that *k'hilah* is more than a onetime gathering. It is the ongoing process of community-building.

Alter's reference to the well-known midrash on the words "and I shall dwell among *them*," drives home the point. God's presence is not contained in a building, but is felt within the intentionally formed community. As Alter has it, *tzivah HaShem sheyakhilu atzmam*, as Israel builds toward holiness, God finds a home in their midst. The point is further made by reference to Moses Alshikh (1508–1593) who writes, "It is *only* by means of the *building* of the Mikdash that I come to dwell, *truly*, amongst the Jewish people."[9] For Alshikh as for Alter, God's "dwelling" in the midst of God's people is the result of their creating a community of purpose. Not the product itself, but the *process* that creates it, is the seat of power.

And what of the Sabbath? Having connected *Mishkan* and *k'hilah*, Alter now turns to Shabbat, seeing it too as a powerful force. Specifically, it is the concentration of all of the week's energy (the six days representing the four compass points, up and down) into one point. In the same way that a group of people becomes a "community" as they are organized, so does a group of days become a "week" as it points toward its goal.

Thus Shabbat, *Mishkan*, and *k'hilah* are all symbols in Alter's reading of the text. What is more, they are all the *same symbol* (even as they are all manifestations of the *s'firah* of *Malchut* in the Lurianic Kabbalah that underpins *Chasidut*): they stand for "the elevation of the whole Jewish people" (*hitrom'mut K'lal Yisrael*). And that elevated state of being (which we might call, for the purposes of this article, "organized"), is the prerequisite for the arrival of the Divine Presence, known also as *K'nesset Yisrael*.

The physical Tabernacle (which is to say, the "program" of *Parashat Vayak'heil*) cannot be separated from the power by which it comes to be, even as the victories we win through our political work cannot be separated from the relational power that makes them possible. This is clear from the final words. Alter concludes his teaching by quoting from Isaiah 66:1, returning to the earlier theme that God has no need for a house. "Thus said the Eternal One/The heaven is My throne/And the earth is My footstool/Where could you build a house for Me?/What place could serve as My abode?"

And while this is a fitting verse in its own right, we might conjecture that Alter had more than the single verse in mind. Just three weeks earlier (when Rosh Chodesh Adar fell on Shabbat T'rumah) he had heard the entire chapter in synagogue. Consider its penultimate verse, spoken twice in the liturgical setting (so as to end with *divrei n'chemta):* "And new moon after new moon/And sabbath after sabbath/All flesh shall come to worship Me/said the Eternal One" (Isa. 66:23).

Sabbath after Sabbath. *Kiddush* after *Kiddush*. Meeting after meeting. Hand held at the shivah home after hand held at the hospice bed. This is where *k'hilah* is created, and *k'hilah* is the prerequisite for real power. Prophetic utterances from the pulpit have a role in today's rabbinate. But they are no substitute for the long, hard work of building relationships, which are the real source of our organizational power. It is those relationships that turn our synagogues into *heichalot:* storehouses for the power (*hayecholet*) that we must bring if we are to succeed in our public work.

Notes

1. I am grateful to Rabbis Alan Henkin and Sanford Ragins, both of whom remember hearing Coffin tell the story, including the memorable punch line.
2. In the lexicon of congregation-based community organizing as taught and practiced by the Industrial Areas Foundation (IAF), "relational power" is set in opposition to "unilateral power." Relational power, or the power inherent in relationships, is built through intentional meetings between two people ("one-to-ones") or in small groups ("house meetings").
3. Robert Linthicum, *Transforming Power: Biblical Strategies for Making a Difference in Your Community* (Downers Grove, IL: InterVarsity Press, 2003), 152.
4. John Emerich Edward Dalberg-Acton, *Essays on Freedom and Power* (Boston: The Beacon Press, 1949), 364. Acton, a faithful Catholic, wrote the words in 1887, in reference to the doctrine of papal infallibility.
5. On the community organizing roots of the civil rights movement in particular, see Charles M. Payne, *I've Got the Light of Freedom: The Organizing Tradition and the Mississippi Freedom Struggle* (Berkeley: University of California, 1995). Through exhaustive archival research, Payne convincingly demonstrates that the civil rights movement was built in local institutions (primarily churches) and not through the charismatic national figures. Cesar Chavez *was* a charismatic national figure with the United Farm Workers, which he built using the principles and strategies he learned organizing with Saul Alinsky and Fred Ross for Community Service Organization (CSO), the IAF's California organization in the 1950s.
6. To be clear: I am not suggesting that Alter had community organizing on his mind when he taught the Chasidim of Ger. My interpretation of his teaching is self-consciously, a work of eisegesis.

7. Yehuda Aryeh Leib Alter, *Sefat Emet* (1905 and subsequent editions). All of Alter's works, including his commentaries on the Pentateuch; many tractates of Talmud; and *Shulchan Aruch, Yoreh Dei-ah*, are known as *Sefat Emet,* after Prov. 12:19, "Lips that speak truth shall be established forever, but a lying tongue is only for a moment." Alter concluded his December 1904 teaching on *Parashat Va-y'chi*—a brief meditation on the power of *Sh'ma Yisrael*—with this prooftext; it proved to be his last public teaching, and he died on January 11, 1905. His son, Avraham Mordecai Alter, succeeded him as Gerer Rebbe and bestowed upon him the name Sefat Emet.
8. *Sefat Emet* is organized by the weekly portion, and within each portion by year.
9. Moses Alshikh, *Torat Mosheh* on Exodus 25:8.

Where the Sanctuary and the Public Square Meet: The Story of Temple Israel's "Vote No on One" Campaign[1]

Stephanie D. Kolin

During the 2008 national election, there was a highly religious presidential candidate's forum at an Evangelical megachurch called Saddleback. Around the same time, thirty-three pastors decided to challenge the IRS by endorsing a presidential candidate in their Sunday sermons. Meanwhile, during the lead up to the election itself, presidential and vice presidential candidates were asked questions like: Do you believe in Creation? Does God take sides in the war on terror? Do you believe that every word of the Bible is factual? Have you ever felt the presence of the holy spirit? And the candidates and their running mates themselves were broadcast nationally, invoking God's name.

With the climate of public life today, we're wise to be wary when politics and religion dress up as each other or intermingle for too long at the party. "God" and "prayer" and "religion" can be words stripped of their sublimity when they are used to claim an absolute moral truth when employed in the public square. We may feel uneasy when a candidate or party claims God is on their side or uses their religious identity to garner votes or as a proof text for being right. The political realm is complicated and colored in shades of

---

RABBI STEPHANIE D. KOLIN (NY06) served Temple Israel of Boston post ordination. She is a co-founder of the Jewish Funds for Justice Rabbinical and Cantorial Student Fellowship for Leadership in Public Life, which trains rabbinical students across the Jewish movements in the arts of Congregation Based Community Organizing. Stephanie is now the California Lead Organizer for the URJ's Just Congregations, working with Reform congregations and rabbis as well as students on the HUC Los Angeles campus.

grey and some might argue that it would be better to leave politics in the public square and the sacred in the sanctuary.

In this article, I examine the challenges that we face in discerning the proper role for synagogues to play within the political sphere while we as rabbis, our lay leaders, and the institutions to which we are connected pursue effective social justice, systemic social change, and our greatest attempts at relevancy in the lives of our congregants. What is at stake when we challenge the often self-imposed and stark divisions between synagogues and the political sphere? And what do we risk when we make the judgment to challenge those divisions in order to powerfully address suffering in the lives of our community members? In this article, I will argue that as rabbis, we are charged with the dual responsibilities of protecting the sacred spaces and opportunities within our congregations and, without painting this as oppositional, also making our legitimate claim as a holy and powerful place where the people gather with the potential to act around values and issues that are significant and meaningful to their and our lives.

Perhaps the best place to begin this discussion is through an examination of the concept of the congregation as apart from the political world—as a sanctuary. "Sanctuary," from the Latin *sanctus*, or holy, came to mean not just a sacred space, but in the Middle Ages, also the protection from the outside world that one might find in that space. A person "seeking sanctuary" from arrest, exile, or persecution would find it, unsurprisingly, in the sanctuary. There is no doubt that some members of our congregations show up for Shabbat or holiday services seeking just such a refuge, a protection from the outside world and the stresses of everyday life, a place to escape the swirling chaos that so often accosts us "out there" so we can find our center "in here." As rabbis, it is wise, then, to recognize that engaging in politics within the walls of the sanctuary may be jarring, scary, infuriating, or confusing to some of our members, just as it may be for some of us to watch the sometimes unholy dance between the two unfold on CNN. But, as rabbis, it is also our responsibility to challenge the false dichotomy between the sanctuary and the public square, challenge the erroneous and even detrimental assumption that engaging in politics as a Reform Jewish congregation is not itself part of the *sanctus* unfolding alongside the holiness of ritual and prayer.

Even as complicated as the political sphere may be, even as you may be reading this while mentally listing the myriad ways that engaging in politics within or as a synagogue is risky and potentially even illegal or unwise as a challenge to the separation of church and state that we maintain is a positive force in this country, I believe that we avoid the complications that arise when the sanctuary and the public square meet at our own peril and to the detriment of our own religious tradition. As difficult as it may be to engage in the political world within the context of sacred ritual life, we and our congregations must be players in this tangle of worlds or we risk betraying our own tradition as a prophetic movement committed to effecting real social change in the world. At risk is nothing less than an admission that synagogues are at best disconnected from, and at worst, irrelevant to the everyday lives of our members. As our congregants and our faith partners in other communities face real pain due to injustices of law, policy, lack of government protection, or because they are particularly vulnerable members of society, we, as Reform Jews, are charged to respond to these injustices by taking actions that can address this pain effectively. I believe that the most effective form of social justice is that which can address issues systemically, powerfully, and with the long-term solutions that can be won only by engaging in the work of social change in the political realm, in the public square. There is, in fact, no better place to engage in the holy work of justice and social change than the space that we separate out as sacred.

And so, as rabbis, we are tasked with answering this question: Is compassion a feeling or is it an action and if it is an action, then can politics truly be left to the public square and sacred things to the sanctuary? As we begin to answer these questions, we also need to develop a language that belongs to us, belongs to our congregations, and lives comfortably in the sacred realm, for if we are to mix religion and politics in this way—acting as a Jewish community in the political arena—it is in our hands to do so responsibly so that we do not feel or cause that queasy, uneasy, manipulative feeling as when God's name is invoked in an interview on the evening news or used as a weapon in a political battle.

Perhaps our response to these questions begins with redefining this burdened and laden word: "politics." Seeking my etymological sources on that height of intellectual discourse, Google, contrary to alarmingly popular belief, the word "politics" does *not* break down into the word poly, meaning "many" and tics, meaning "blood-sucking creatures." The word "politics" comes from the Greek word "polis," meaning city or body of citizens, and the polis in Athens was the central place where citizens came to do business, to conduct negotiations, and to make shared decisions about their lives—polis as public square. The problem with politics, pastor and teacher Brian McLaren writes, "is when politics comes to mean 'dirty politics' or 'partisan politics' or 'narrow, wedge-issue, litmus-test, culture-wars politics.'"[2] Because before it means any of those things, it means people meeting face to face to make decisions about their lives rather than passively flying through space and time in isolation. The opportunity to reclaim the concept of politics as a place where individuals meet, know one another, respond to one another, truly see one another, and negotiate fairly with one another to influence the direction that their own society will take, is in the hands of the people when the people choose to gather in the polis. Politics in its true and simplest form, is, then, neutral; it's a forum through which we may respond to injustice. For whatever it has come to mean derisively, politics is merely a tool of engagement and, one could argue, the arena in which our communities can act most effectively on the issues and values at the heart of our congregations.

This may be easy to swallow in the theoretical, but what happens when the rubber hits the road and the theoretical becomes the very real? The following story is not one with simple answers or obvious conclusions, but rather will hopefully offer an opportunity to grapple with the narrative of a political campaign taking place within the walls of a sanctuary and the questions and challenges that emerged from taking seriously our charge to enact justice and act powerfully for social change, even when the decision to do so is complicated.

Temple Israel and the Vote No on One Campaign

Temple Israel is a 1,700-family congregation, the largest Reform synagogue in New England, and has a long history of and commitment to engaging in social justice through Congregation Based Community Organizing. This is a grass roots model of systemic social change work in which the issues addressed within the community come out of a practice called one-to-one or relational meetings in which community members choose to sit with one another and share their stories, experiences, and the pain with which they struggle in their lives. Those members then have the opportunity to act as leaders, alongside interfaith partners with shared concerns, in campaigns to effect change within the public square. Temple Israel members have engaged in and celebrated victories in campaigns on affordable housing, education, equal marriage, transgender rights, and an anti-bullying curriculum. Temple members also played a critical role in the campaign to win near universal healthcare in the Commonwealth of Massachusetts, a flagship model as the country now turns toward the creation of a national healthcare system. Reform congregations across the country are now engaging in this kind of work with great political success, a deepening of relationships within their congregations and between their members and their interfaith partners, and strengthening their communities with the guidance and support from Just Congregations, an arm of the Union for Reform Judaism, founded and directed by Rabbi Jonah Pesner, who has helped rabbis and lay leaders to experiment with this model of systemic social justice work and relational culture.[3]

Temple Israel is a member congregation of the Greater Boston Interfaith Organization (GBIO),[4] our local broad-based organization, which brings together fifty-five churches, synagogues, mosques, and several other community institutions, to act powerfully on local issues of injustice, and has a twelve-year history of engaging in systemic social change work through the model of Congregation Based Community Organizing.

During spring 2008, Massachusetts citizens learned that the November ballot would include a statewide question that, if passed, would ban the Massachusetts state income tax. The consequences of voter approval would wipe out $12.7 billion in revenue, representing 40 percent of the state budget, eliminating funding for education, public safety, services for seniors, youth, and people with disabilities, and the near universal healthcare gains for which Temple Israel had fought so hard in previous years and continued to work to protect.

Out of these thousands of conversations, house meetings, and the depth of our relationships within Temple Israel and other GBIO member congregations, we knew that the losses that would follow the banning of the state income tax would deeply hurt our members and our brothers and sisters across the Greater Boston area. And we also knew that the threat was very real. Only a few years earlier, this same question nearly passed with 46 percent of the vote.

An organization of allies across Massachusetts formed and developed a strategy in which participating communities would collect pledge cards on which an individual would pledge to go to the polls on Election Day and vote no to this ballot question, which was now known as "Question 1." GBIO called a Delegates Assembly, a gathering of leaders from each member congregation, to gauge whether or not this campaign was in the interest of our members, whether we had the capacity to take it on, and whether this issue was important enough to our membership to do the hard work it would take to defeat Question 1. In that meeting, GBIO decided to engage in this campaign and we made a commitment to collect sixteen thousand pledge cards, representing a significant voter turnout and the largest commitment from any organization within the Commonwealth of Massachusetts.

It then became critical for Temple Israel's social justice leaders to decide where we stood and whether we, as a congregation, would join with our umbrella organization in this particular campaign. Social justice at Temple Israel is guided by an extremely talented group of temple members, some who have been doing this for twelve years and some who had joined the community just a few months earlier. This team represents the diversity of Temple Israel, including members from our twenties and thirties group; board members; parents of high school kids, pre-school kids, and middle school kids; members who are gay, lesbian, transgender, and bisexual; seniors; single folks; Jews; and non-Jews. Community organizing at Temple Israel is called Ohel Tzedek (Tent of Justice) as we seek to not exist as a closed team or committee structure, but rather as a mode by which we act with every door (or tent flap) open to anyone who wishes to engage. And the Ohel Tzedek Leadership Team now had a challenging task before them.

Over the summer, we held an emergency meeting to discuss our options. We could decide not to take on this complicated campaign and step back from this political moment or we could decide to engage and figure out what it would mean to do so. There are several issues an organizing team must consider at a moment like this. Is the issue we are considering one that is broadly felt within our community—meaning, do a lot of people care about it? Is it an issue that is deeply felt—meaning, do a lot of people care about it *a lot*? Is it winnable? Is there specific action to take? Will it affect the balance of power in the larger society? Will it develop new leadership along the way? Is this issue divisive? Around a couple of pizzas and a box of clementines, we asked ourselves these questions in order to discern the right next step for our community.

The Ohel Tzedek leaders considered the stories we had heard from our members in one-on-one and small group meetings during the past years about their worries over not being able to take care of their aging parents and their concerns for the safety of their children and the resulting need for youth programs. We discussed the hard work that Temple Israel had done on the Massachusetts healthcare campaign, on affordable housing, and other areas that would completely lose their funding if Question 1 were to pass. We relayed conversations we'd had with members who had disabled children at home and needed services to help them, and we inquired within the larger community through our network of relationships.

Were these issues broadly felt? Yes. Were they felt deeply in the guts of our families? Yes. Could we win this campaign? If we worked hard enough, quickly enough, strategically enough, and with our faith partners, then, we believed, yes we could. The complicated question of whether this issue would be divisive for our community remained, but we also knew that we would not know the answer to that question until we began to act. (We would be able to discern at least part of the answer through the reactions of our community, which was not a small risk to take, but one that we deemed worth it.) Furthermore, the specter of losing the services, programs, and funding behind the issues that reflected Temple Israel's work and the values at the heart of our community and the communities of our brothers and sisters across Greater Boston, was a powerful and driving force. With no small amount of strategic thinking, commitment to our relationships within and without of Temple Israel, and a desire to protect our families, we were compelled to join with GBIO in the campaign that was now known as "Vote No on Question 1."

Deciding to engage in a campaign is not the same as working out how to engage effectively. We knew we would gather pledge cards at various community functions in and outside the walls of Temple Israel, at Shabbat services, Torah study, religious school, etc., but there was a significant and people-packed moment in the Jewish calendar quickly approaching and the potential for action in that space and the very public and sacred nature of it did not escape us. See, the summer was ending and the High Holy Days were quickly approaching. We knew that in the month of September, somewhere between four thousand and five thousand Temple Israel members would be coming through our doors—a far greater number than at any other time during the year. The opportunity to engage the largest swath of our congregation in this work and to give our members a chance to act for justice in the middle of the High Holy Days was quite compelling. Collecting pledge cards during Rosh HaShanah services was an exciting possibility, but not an uncomplicated one.

We could have simply decided that I would deliver a sermon about the Vote No on 1 campaign, since I, like many Reform rabbis, enjoy the privilege of having freedom of the pulpit. Yet we knew that effective justice work in the public square is not about the singular act of a rabbi from the bimah. It is about the engagement of a body of organized people who come together to act powerfully on issues of shared concern. Thankfully, the weight of a single sermon pales in comparison to what the voice and actions of the people can accomplish.

Our team immediately got to work bringing interested leaders into the action, collecting cards in all the places that our members and extended Temple Israel family gather. More than thirty members new to community organizing got involved in collecting these pledge cards, learning to tell their personal story about how this vote would affect their own life and the lives of their children or parents. Our teens got excited about the campaign and learned the art of community organizing through phone banking and canvassing local neighborhoods, sharing their commitment to critical programming in public schools and programs for physically and learning disabled students. As we did our work, so did members of our allied churches, mosques, and other synagogues. Meanwhile, our Ohel Tzedek Leadership Team began preparing a presentation for our Temple Israel executive board to open a conversation with them about collecting pledge cards at Rosh HaShanah, which, as a temple-wide gathering, could be seen as representative of the community as a whole and so called for the serious thinking of the appointed leaders of our community.

Navigating the Challenges Together

Over the next weeks, Temple Israel's executive board, the clergy, and the Ohel Tzedek Leadership Team began to navigate the significant questions around engaging the full congregation and acting as Temple Israel in the public square, or the political realm. There were three main questions that arose around the possibility of collecting pledge cards in the sanctuary during the High Holy Days. First, would weighing in publicly on a campaign to defeat a ballot initiative put the synagogue's 501(c)(3) status as a nonprofit at risk? Second, could a perception of this action as a partisan issue be divisive in our community, alienating people on one of the holiest days of the year? And third, and clearly most critically, do politics belong in the sanctuary on the High Holy Days, or was this a campaign that should take place only *outside* the sanctuary and *outside* the High Holy Days, both in time and space? This last question was the most central to our conversation and remains the most central to this discourse: Does political engagement toward the goal of social change and justice contradict, challenge, or threaten the sacred space of our congregations? Does congregational political action exist outside the realm of sacred ritual or is there a way that we can imagine it as part of a whole? In short, what happens when the sanctuary and the public square meet?

We were able to address the question of tax status with a quick phone call to the Religious Action Center, which assured us that only public support of a specific candidate, not a ballot question, would call our IRS status into question.

We took the question of the potential divisiveness of the campaign very seriously. Even though legislators on both sides of the aisle wanted to see Question 1 defeated, Temple Israel, like most Reform congregations, represents the complete spectrum of political affiliation, and a ballot question that deals with taxing the people could be seen as favoring a liberal agenda. An important principle of community organizing is to avoid issues or campaigns that are divisive, because the goal of acting together is to increase the power of the civic sector and taking on issues that divide the people would clearly make us less powerful. As a religious community, we are also charged with making sure that we are a spiritual home to everyone regardless of their political affiliations and as we negotiate our engagement in the public square, it is on us to not make our members feel like outsiders. We felt committed to making sure all voices could be heard and so, with the wise advice of our senior rabbi, Rabbi Ronne Friedman, we decided to revise the pledge card that we were using at Temple Israel by adding another check-box to the original text. The options for signing the card were now three: "I think this is an important issue and I want to get more involved," "I pledge to vote no on Question 1," and now, "I disagree with this issue and want to speak with someone about it." While this may seem like a simple or small addition, if we are to negotiate the interaction of the political and religious realms, then it is our task to engage in political work within our congregations responsibly, which means making sure that each person's voice is heard and valued, that no one should feel like an outsider in their own spiritual home.

It is the third question, of the intersection between the sanctuary and the public square, however, that is the driving force behind this article and is a central issue in so many of our congregations as we struggle to engage in authentic, effective, powerful social justice work while keeping intact the integrity of what it means to be a religious institution and a sacred space. Perhaps, as rabbis, we are seen as guardians of the right of our congregants to escape the mundane goings on of the outside world by seeking comfort within the protective walls of their sanctuary. Perhaps we see ourselves as primarily pastor, preacher, and protector, carving out a space of quiet reflection on the holiest days of our Jewish year. But our tradition challenges us loudly regarding the use of our prayer spaces.

The Sanctuary and the Public Square Meet

Rabbi Hiyya ben Abba says in the name of Rabbi Yochanan: "A person should not pray *elah b'vayit she'yesh sham chalonot*, save for in a room which has windows, as it says: 'And the windows of his upper chamber were open toward Jerusalem (Daniel 6:11).' Rav Kahana says: 'A person who prays in a valley is brazen.'"[5] The law code, *Shulchan Aruch*, expands upon both of these Talmudic statements.[6] Regarding the charge that one is to pray in a room that has windows, the Talmud develops the idea further, explaining that these windows should open toward Jerusalem. Regarding the text warning against praying in a valley, it is interpreted to mean that one should not pray outside in an open field.

From these simple halachic statements, we can mine a world of meaning as we encounter our holy spaces and risk redefining them within the context of our own inherited traditions. There are several commentaries that attempt to more deeply understand these two related, but different, regulations when it comes to the physical place in which we pray. *Talmidei Rabbeinu Yonah* offers that the reason we must have windows that face Jerusalem is, in fact, that we should be focusing our prayerful attention on Jerusalem itself as each Jew turns to form a vast circle around the site of the Temple, making concrete a wistful mourning for a geographical center. Rashi comes to offer a different interpretation, suggesting that looking out at the grandeur of the heavens subdues one's heart to God, reminding the pray-er that he or she is not calling all the shots. Commenting on why we shouldn't pray in open spaces, Rashi teaches that open areas can inspire feelings of excessive freedom and, therefore, arrogance. As he tries to strike a balance between these two statements, Rashi invites us to wonder about how we achieve both the sense of awe in the transcendent that prayer can generate inside us and also the grounded reality of the immanent world and the humbling notion that we are not ourselves omnipotent beings. We, too, live in the vacillations between the transcendence and immanence of prayer and the experience of praying it.

As Reform rabbis, we are charged with learning from this chain of tradition and adding our own voices to this unfolding interpretation as our present-day realities call for its responsible application to our own particular circumstances, challenges, and needs. And so perhaps we can offer that if we are to pray in a room that has windows, and those windows are specifically built to face Jerusalem, then a certain physical orientation is created that affects the words in our mouths and the implications of taking them seriously. As we know, midrash points our bodies toward Jerusalem when we pray[7] and in the *Shulchan Aruch*, the halachah places windows directly before us, carving out a portal to the outside world even while we are in the midst of prayer.

When Rabbi Joseph Karo was crafting this law in his legal code, casting our eyes outward toward the world, on what did he imagine our eyes might fall? If we were to gaze upward, we might feel the awe of dwelling in a world where God dwells; if we gaze outward, we might feel the awe of being part of a sacred network of other human beings. Upward and we catch a glimpse of the potential we have to be our best selves. Outward and we catch a glimpse of the arena in which it matters if we act as our best selves. The interplay between inside and outside, personal and public space, the womb-like security of the walls and the light of the world streaming in through the glass invite us to redefine the meaning of sanctuary and the activities that are worthy of being called sacred when enacted within those walls.

And yet, in the same breath, our tradition charges us not to pray in an open field. As generations of Jewish campers sitting by lakes and praying in fields gasp in disbelief, we can find meaning in these words as well. Valleys and fields may be seen as dangerous when it comes to prayerfulness because they themselves have no boundaries and, as in the story above, the political world is complicated and runs the risk of also being a sphere with no boundaries. There is no place for a political free for all, abusive words, or partisan politics in the midst of *t'filah*. In fact there are boundaries, and while I would not deign to claim that I know them all, I would challenge the Reform rabbinate that it is on us to discover them, test them, engage them, and ultimately define them so that the sanctuaries that we create, those in which we lead prayer and engage in justice, are places that we can authentically continue to call sacred, even as we look out those profoundly curious windows and imagine all that we are called to do.

So with all of the challenges involved, why not leave politics in the public square and the sacred in the sanctuary? Well, our sanctuaries have windows and we are charged to gaze out of them even as we gaze inward in prayer. And so the question falls to us in this present day: Can we be satisfied if our ritual moments allow us only to gaze upward and inward, but don't also call us to gaze outward? In the current economic crisis, as financial institutions gain an unwieldy amount of power and our families are struggling and our partners in other faith communities are suffering, we are charged by our own reflections in the window panes: Can a Jewish community witness and not react? We find ourselves asking the most eternal of Jewish questions as we return to this thought: is compassion a feeling, or is it an action?

We know, too, that we are not the first generation of Jewish communities to be asking these questions. The High Holy Days themselves, of course, present us with a paradigm in which ritual and justice are intertwined, challenge one another, and call the lack of the other into question. Isaiah 58, our often quoted, yet unendingly profound Yom Kippur haftarah, offers us a relevant worldview as we take up these questions. In the text, God informs Isaiah: "To be sure, these people seek Me daily, eager to learn My ways. They ask Me for the right way, they are eager for *kirbat elohim* [drawing near to God]." But, as we know, the Israelites don't really achieve the closeness to the Divine that they desire. God calls them out for praying and fasting with fervor, all the while worrying about their businesses and oppressing their laborers. God decries that they fast amid conflict and contention as if their ritual and their daily life don't affect one another. In short, God challenges our ancestral community, saying: "You've got no windows in your sanctuary!" Enter Isaiah, who comes to blast a window in the side of their Temple.

It may be tempting to dismiss these Judeans as lost in their own excesses and unrelated to our own lives, but even a cursory reading of their transgressions tells a story that resonates for most of us. Who are these Judeans? These are the people who show up for services, filling the Temple with prayer. Yes, the text tells us that they oppress their workers, make unethical choices, are distracted in prayer, even intimating that they ignore the hungry and naked in their midst, yet these are the people who show up. They are the imperfect and beautiful and tumultuous souls standing before God within the walls of their sanctuary around the year 515 B.C.E. Has that much really changed or are these Judeans simply an earlier iteration of the makeup of our own communities? Are not we ourselves and our own imperfections reflected in their words?

While according to our text they seem genuine in their attempt to engage with God, they are so unaware of or unwilling to engage in what's happening outside the walls of the rebuilt Temple that they end up adding to the problems of society rather than fixing them. While one could argue that they are, in fact, singularly engaged in what's going on outside the walls of the Temple (their own business practice, their laborers, their profits), we know that these Judeans are seeing clearly neither the pain they are causing nor their responsibility to address it.

So God tells them—here, this is what your prayer and fasting need to look like: "unlock the unjust shackles, untie the cords of the yoke, free the oppressed and break off every yoke on every neck. Share your bread with the hungry. When you see the naked, clothe him, and do not ignore your own kin." God doesn't tell the people to pray for repair of these injustices or to pray and then go do them. Prayer and fasting and *kirbat elohim* are described as one and the same thing. The "fast" that God asks for surely includes ritual, but is also defined by acts of justice and compassion as the ritual world intermingles with and indeed becomes synonymous with taking real action in the public square. Our text, then, offers us a call to notice what's going on outside the window and a call to respond. God charges these Judeans: *shalach r'tzutzim chofshim*, free the oppressed. *R'tzutzim*, oppressed, also means "crushed." Charged not just to feed one person or clothe one individual, sacred acts of *chesed* themselves, these Temple-going Judeans are to "uncrush" oppressed souls. God challenges them and in turn us: Can a Jewish community witness and not react? Is compassion a feeling, or is it an action?

While we may not demonstrate the same malaise as our Judean ancestors, we are the people of faith in our day, trying to engage with the ethereal realm and attempting to figure out what it means to be the people Israel today. And so we also have the opportunity to decide what it means to look out the window and respond to what we see—to uncrush the crushed. And when what we see is suffering not just outside our window or across the world, but also just across the sanctuary itself, we have to ask loudly and often and of one another: can politics be left to the public square and sacred things to the sanctuary?

A couple of months before the Vote No on Question One campaign began, a woman stood up in the sanctuary of Temple Emanuel, a Conservative congregation in Newton, Massachusetts, and told her community that her mother was now homebound and was begging her not to make her go into a residence. She shared that she so wanted to do right by her mother, but the current legislation affecting the lives of seniors and their care was making it nearly impossible to keep her at home. She sincerely thanked everyone for their acts of profound *chesed*, for visiting her, for bringing food to her mother, for calling, but said that the greatest act of *chesed* they could offer would be to help her work to change the laws so it would be possible for her to honor her mother and keep her at home. She is crushed under a weight that she cannot lift alone. In this story and so many others like it, we find that religion and politics are indeed able to meet in the sanctuary. Or was that the public square? Perhaps sanctuary and square are not so separate when their reflections meet in the window pane.

One can imagine similar reflections in the window panes of other synagogues—as well as mosques and churches. In the case of Vote No on 1, we were dealing with a campaign that had a clear end—Election Day 2008—but the suffering within our communities as houses are foreclosed upon, people are losing their jobs, families and students are carrying an egregious amount of debt, and interest rates are still underregulated, compels Christian, Muslim, and Jewish communities to continue gazing out our windows, trying to hear and interpret the words of God and our sacred texts and, therefore, our responsibilities to one another. At our best, we do not engage in political campaigns just as a single Jewish community, because when we look out the windows of our sanctuary, there is standing a Christian woman who is suffering under the huge debt that she carries and there is standing a Muslim man whose bank is foreclosing on his home and there stands our partners as we enter the public square.

The issues at the heart of our congregations and the actions required to make real social change call us into the polis to meet, to talk, to negotiate, and to act powerfully and politically. And our tradition calls us to truly hear one another, to respond to the pain that we hear, and to work together to repair the brokenness that is revealed by those stories. Enacting justice has never been simple nor is it so today, but we have the opportunity to rewrite, recraft, and redefine the concept of politics, not in its corrupted form, but as that central place where citizens meet to reflect on and make shared decisions about their lives. And as the Reform rabbinate of our day, we have the opportunity to redefine the role of the synagogue community and reimagine our capacity for social change and political power. We are imagining and indeed creating congregations where our members truly know one another, see one another, and share publicly our stories of struggle and then learning the tools we need to be able to act together in the most effective and sacred way to address the pain we see in each others' eyes and hear in each others' words. Our task is nothing short of engaging in politics in such a way that makes political work holy and engaging in prayer in such a way that makes our ritual an act of justice.

Be Afraid and Pray…

As most complicated but worthwhile stories will, our Vote No on 1 story ends with many successes, many challenges, and a few more questions. With the wisdom, commitment, passion, and courage of our clergy team, senior staff, our board of trustees, our social justice leaders, and with guidance from allies in the Greater Boston Interfaith Organization and the Jewish Community Relations Council of Boston, Temple Israel ultimately did engage our congregation during Rosh HaShanah in the Vote No on One Campaign. A pledge card was placed on each seat and an announcement was made at the end of each service by a rabbi. We explained a bit about the ballot question and asked our members to consider how they would vote. We let them know that if they intended to vote no, we'd like to know about that and add them to our count. And we also told them that if they disagreed with this campaign and wanted to speak to someone about it, then they should check that box.

Temple Israel members ended up collecting over 1,700 pledge cards and through our work, GBIO, and the coalition of allies throughout Greater Boston, the Vote No on Question 1 campaign was overwhelmingly victorious. We defeated Question 1 with 60 percent of the vote, making the voice of the people unquestionably heard and guaranteeing protection for the programs and funding on which they rely. Throughout this campaign, there were other successes, including the development of new leaders within Temple Israel and the Ohel Tzedek Leadership Team becoming a stronger group of leaders, more deeply in relationship with one another, and therefore, more powerful as a team. The healthy tension and struggle that emerged from the conversations with Temple Israel leadership and staff opened new doors of possibility and also significantly deepened those relationships as well.

Some challenges certainly emerged. Some members were offended by our engagement in political action in the sanctuary during the High Holy Days. About five members checked off the box indicating disagreement with the issue and three of those chose to speak with me. While these were not easy conversations, they were, in fact, quite rich and opened new opportunities for relationships, conversation, and mutual respect between congregants and clergy. There's no doubt in my mind that we did not do everything "right," but what we learned through this work was invaluable.

The greatest "win," however, was, perhaps, the opportunity for engagement in the critical questions of this political moment. The Reform Movement has a long and beautiful and powerful tradition of responding to the prophetic voice in the most effective ways possible. Today, we have the opportunity to organize ourselves, partner with other faith communities, truly hear one another's stories, and hold our elected officials accountable to the issues and values that are most central to the lives of our members and our families.

Will these questions ever be simple? Probably not. And most likely, they never should feel simple because if we do become flippant, if we do allow hubris or carelessness to be our guiding principles, then we will no doubt have slipped into the patterns of those who abuse religious language and belief in the public square to manipulate others or claim God as singularly on their side. There is great risk in taking on the responsibility of engaging in systemic justice work within our sacred spaces. Rabbi Abraham Joshua Heschel tells the story of a person who was asked to lead prayer for his community. Anxious about this daunting task, he approached his rabbi, the Rabbi of Husiatin, and explained that he was afraid to pray.[8] He was afraid he'd get the words wrong. He was afraid God wouldn't accept his prayer because of his unworthiness. He was afraid he would lead his community astray. He was afraid and looking for answers. His rabbi answered him, saying "be afraid and pray." And perhaps the Rabbi of Husiatin wouldn't mind if we borrow his language as we offer ourselves the same, although slightly expanded advice. Be afraid and yet still pray. Be afraid and yet still act. It is a great risk to intertwine our sacred spaces and our ritual times with political action, yet it is an even greater risk not to. It is a greater risk to allow others to define what is right and good and it is a greater risk to allow our acts of ritual and our acts of justice to drift so far apart from one another that our congregations can find relevance in neither. It is the greatest risk to look out of our windows and refuse to see either the suffering in our world or the potential we have to heal it.

We will not always get this right, but if we do our work through deep relationships with others, if we do our work thoughtfully and with integrity, compassion, wisdom, and not a little strategic thinking, then it will be worth it to engage in even the most complicated and challenging questions about what it means to act as a Jewish community in the public square. It will be worth it every time a person who felt powerless and crushed finds his or her voice and acts with others as part of his or her Jewish community. It will be worth it every time members feel heard and seen within their Jewish community and, looking to their right and left, truly know the people next to which they pray and act. It will be worth it every time a campaign in our congregations leads to the passage of a piece of legislation that protects a vulnerable part of our community and the communities of our faith partners. It will be worth it every time a member of one of our congregations takes ownership over the work and becomes a leader for justice in a way she or he never imagined was possible. And it will be worth it when the redemptive verses of Exodus and the voice of the Prophet Isaiah intermingle with our voices in the sanctuary and at the state house, judiciary committees, the White House, and every place in which the people gather to alter the balance of power in society and to do the work of effective, systemic, sacred justice.

Notes

1. I want to offer my deepest thanks to my teachers, organizers, and friends who offered invaluable guidance on the original Rosh HaShanah sermon I wrote in 2008 from which the idea for this article came and on this article itself, in particular Lila Foldes, Dana Gershon, Reverend Hurmon Hamilton, Meir Lakien, and Rabbi Jonah Pesner.
2. Brian McLaren, "What Do You Mean by Politics?" blogging on http://blog.beliefnet.com/godspolitics/2008/06/what-do-you-mean-by-politics-p-1.html, June 5, 2008.
3. Find more information about Just Congregations at the Union for Reform Judaism Web site, http://urj.org/socialaction/training/justcongregations/.
4. Find more information about GBIO at www.GBIO.org.
5. BT *B'rachot* 34b.
6. *Shulchan Aruch Orach Chaim* 90:4.
7. BT *B'rachot* 30a.
8. Abraham Joshua Heschel, *Man Is Not Alone* (New York: Farrar, Straus and Giroux, 1951), 256.

Poetry

For Yaakov Ari Ringler

Stanley Chyet z"l

Jacob
it's a time of noise
a time of shriekings and stammerings
you come to now

Jacob
roar

Jacob
give a meaning to this time

Jacob
you will wrestle

Jacob
you will limp

roar, Jacob
give your meaning
to this time

RABBI STANLEY CHYET, Ph.D. (C57), who lived from 1931–2002, is remembered as one of the most beloved and admired professors at the Hebrew Union College, from which he also took his B.H.L., M.A., and Ph.D. His relationship with his students was distinguished by the extraordinary respect he demonstrated and interest expressed in each one of us. His patience as a teacher and his enthusiasm for our own particular intellectual and spiritual journeys was affirming, particularly since his approach, at the time, was *yotzei dofen*. Indeed, for many of us Stanley was not only a mentor but also a caring friend. I was in Stanley's Hebrew class during my first year in the then joint HUC–UC program in 1960. This was also Stanley's first year on faculty.

POETRY

Over the years our friendship bloomed in part due to common interests and concerns. Progressive politics and Labor Zionism were noteworthy areas of shared conviction and preoccupation. Not surprisingly Stanley and sometimes Gerri and children visited with us in our places of residence. He was with us in Miami, where I served as regional Hillel director, when my first child was born in 1973. Just a few days before Yaakov's *b'rit milah*, Stanley presented us with this poem, which he read at the ceremony. Recently, after many years of searching we rediscovered the poem among Yaakov's personal papers. The poem was written in a time of great social and political upheaval. We were preoccupied and engaged as both Americans and Jews. Stanley brilliantly captured the moment by using metaphor and biblical associations to my son's name.

Stanley would have been proud of Yaakov. Having made *aliyah* just weeks after his bar mitzvah, Yaakov went on to graduate high school, learning Hebrew and French and later Arabic. He served in the Israeli Army Intelligence Corps and graduated the Hebrew University in Philosophy and Economics. Later he earned a master's degree in International Policy at Columbia University.

Stanley typed this poem on a piece of my office stationery. Under his initials and the date, he signed it "With love from Stan Chyet." I now offer this poem to readers of the *CCAR Journal* as a memorial to Stanley. — RABBI STANLEY RINGLER (C69).

Shofar

Debra R. Hachen

Thin column of air
(squeezed up from the twin lobes of hope and despair)
passes the larynx.

The old year catches in the throat
as a new year rushes forth
escaping to freedom past vibrating lips
that alternate between control and release.

No holding back.

DEBRA R. HACHEN (NY80) is the rabbi of Temple Beth El of Northern Valley, Closter, New Jersey.

Book Reviews

Just Torah
A Review Essay

Eric Caplan

Reviewing

Whose Torah? A Concise Guide to Progressive Judaism by Rebecca T. Alpert (New York: The New Press, 2008), 164 pp.

Righteous Indignation: A Jewish Call for Justice edited by Or N. Rose, Jo Ellen Green Kaiser, and Margie Klein (Woodstock, VT: Jewish Lights Publishing, 2008), 351 pp.

North American Jews are increasingly interested in doing social justice work in the outside world that is linked in a clear way to their Jewish identities. A variety of factors have converged to foster this interest in activism under Jewish auspices. Many of us believe that the social, political, economic, and environmental situation of the world has reached a critical stage and that things must change if our species is to survive. We expect and need Judaism to address the core challenges that we face as people. Only a Judaism that is deeply engaged with the world can be fully relevant to our lives. We are tired of the narrow focus on internal Jewish issues that characterized Jewish communal life in the 1980s and 1990s. And we are searching for new ways to attract younger Jews who are rejecting traditional paths of communal affiliation and Jewish expression.

How can we insure that the current interest in social justice does not turn out to be a passing fad, subject to the same ebb and flow that saw the heightened levels of Jewish activism of the 1960s give way to the insularity and individualism of the 1980s?

There is no one answer here but it seems clear that we must keep our communities well informed so that Jews are always aware of the great challenges of our times. We need to suggest concrete solutions and provide paths within a Jewish context to contribute to their realization. We must show that outwardly focused social activism is indeed a Jewish imperative, and we must demonstrate how a dialogue with the texts, rituals, and history of the Jewish people can enrich and nurture social justice work. *Whose Torah? A Concise Guide to Progressive Judaism* and *Righteous Indignation: A Jewish Call for Justice* contribute positively to the realization of these goals.

Rebecca T. Alpert—the author of *Whose Torah?*—was ordained by the Reconstructionist Rabbinical College where she also served as dean of students. Alpert is currently associate professor of religion and women's studies at Temple University.

Whose Torah? is part of a series in which "leading thinkers from Judaism, Catholicism, Protestantism, and Islam demonstrate how their traditions call for progressive positions on contemporary issues." Alpert recognizes that parts of the Jewish tradition are not especially progressive, and the book's introduction is devoted to a frank discussion of how to approach these pieces of our heritage. She believes that some of their bite can be moderated by seeing them within the historical reality in which they evolved and by recourse to midrash and other traditional forms of reinterpretation. It is sometimes useful, however, to reject such material outright. Doing so is empowering and can help us to better focus on the life-affirming parts of the tradition. "Ultimately, if we want to be part of the Jewish people, we must turn away from our anger and look for the sources of our tradition that nurture and support our passion for justice" (p. 9). Alpert's own passion was nurtured in early life by studying the biblical prophets and by witnessing rabbis taking a leading role in the civil rights movement of the 1960s. She became a rabbi to follow in their path. Personal revelations like these contribute to making *Whose Torah?* a compelling read.

Alpert's book covers a lot of ground. Separate chapters are devoted to sexuality, gender, race, war and peace, poverty, and the environment, and each chapter deals with many topics. The chapter on sexuality, for example, discusses Judaism's basic attitude to sex; *nidah* and *mikveh*; new Rosh Chodesh ceremonies and other rituals that celebrate women's bodies; gender-based stereotypes; premarital sex; gay, lesbian, and bisexual sexuality; transgender rights; and gay marriage.

This is a short book—in both height and length. Accordingly, much of the book surveys Jewish positions without going into great depth. There are few footnotes and not many in-text citations. Whole sections provide an overview of the work of various Jewish organizations active on a given issue. *Whose Torah?* is addressed to Jews—Alpert uses language like "our Jewish voice needs to be..."—who seek a general understanding of how Jewish progressives are addressing the issues discussed and who may be searching for an organization that reflects their personal views.

This does not mean that there is nothing here for the knowledgeable, involved Jew. Alpert advocates passionately for the causes that she believes in and occasionally puts forth positions that are not commonly heard within the Jewish world. The chapter on race is especially interesting in this regard. Alpert notes that most Jewish efforts on behalf of racial justice are "predicated on the assumption that Jews are white" (p. 75). In reality, up to 20 percent of America's Jews are of North African, Latino, and African descent. She arrives at this high figure by including groups not generally recognized as Jews by the formal community, including Black Hebrews and Israelites. Alpert believes that if we saw ourselves as mixed-race we would be more inclined to view the social, economic, and political challenges facing Africa as *our* challenges; likewise the difficult realities of inner-city life in the United States. This sense of personal connection would help motivate and sustain our activism. If excluding others is unjust, inviting black Jewish synagogues and organizations into our community is a social justice imperative. Although these groups live their Judaism differently than we do, Alpert believes that these differences are no greater than the ones that separated Reform and Orthodox Jews in the nineteenth century or that divide traditional and humanist Jews today. Reading *Whose Torah?* led me to visit Web sites such as www.blackjews.org and www.kingdomofyah.com for the first time. I left wondering if our rejection of these groups is not a function of some unconscious perception of black people as fundamentally "other." There seems to be enough Judaism in these communities for us to engage them in some form of intrafaith dialogue.

Alpert recounts a story from her experience accompanying and supporting women seeking abortions that exposes one of the ways that Jewish ritual can nourish activism. The particular clinic that she was defending performed abortions early on Saturday morning. The antiabortionists who picketed the clinic sought to intimidate the women and the people who were accompanying them. Alpert and her fellow activists were outraged and hurt by what they experienced. To bolster themselves they began to sing sections of the Jewish liturgy that pray for peace. This became an essential part of their weekly routine at the clinic. Alpert writes that by infusing ritual into their activism they claimed "religious grounding" for their viewpoint. This strengthened their resolve to continue their difficult work and also helped them to understand the protestors who stood before them. "We gained the insight that although we stood on opposite sides of this debate, we both took positions from deeply held religious beliefs.... We found this effort helped us understand their humanity and their passion, even as we disagreed" (p. 64).

I found Alpert's presentation of the Jewish perspectives on most of the issues discussed to be balanced and credible. I am less convinced than she is, however, that the Rabbis of the Mishnah and Talmud had a moral objection to wars that the Bible defines as permissible but not obligatory. Much of her argument rests on the Rabbis' complex relationship to Chanukah. Whereas the Hasmoneans celebrated the festival as a glorification of their military achievements, the Rabbis built their celebration around the miracle of the oil. But this shift may not reflect a morally grounded antiwar perspective but rather the volatile political reality in which the Rabbis lived. The Jews paid a heavy price for their revolts against Rome of 66 C.E. and 132 C.E. The Rabbis may have feared that in using Chanukah to glorify a previous Jewish revolt they risked triggering another catastrophic rebellion. Alpert ignores the Al Ha-Nisim prayer in which the Rabbis specifically thank God for the Maccabean wars. It is not possible to read this prayer and share her conclusion that the Hasmonean revolt was "not looked on favorably" (p. 89). This is a minor quibble. On the whole, *Whose Torah?* is a well-written and researched presentation of an impressive array of topics.

Righteous Indignation deals with many of the issues raised in Alpert's book and quite a few that she does not address, such as health care, the justice system, and schooling. The book is an anthology of forty essays, organized under broad headings (e.g., "Creating an Inclusive Community," "The Yoke of Oppression: Social and

Economic Justice"). Each essay is written by different authors, and there are contributions from most of the well-known contemporary non-Orthodox Jewish activists (including Michael Lerner, Arthur Waskow, Ellen Bernstein, David Saperstein, Jonah Pesner, Jill Jacobs, Daniel Sokatch, and Ruth Messinger), as well as selections from a number of people with more modest national profiles (e.g., Sandra M. Fox, chair of the Western Pennsylvania Coalition for Single-Payer Healthcare; Mark Hanis, founder and executive director of the Genocide Intervention Network).

In the introduction, the book's editors—Or N. Rose (associate dean, the Rabbinical School at Hebrew College), Margie Klein (founder and director, Moshe House Boston: Kavod Jewish Social Justice House), and Jo Ellen Green Kaiser (editor in chief, *Zeek: A Journal of Jewish Thought and Culture*)—write that the anthology is aimed at two populations: affiliated Jews who do not engage in social activism and nonaffiliated Jews who do. They hope to convince the former group that social justice work is an integral part of what it means to be a Jew and the latter one that "the religious teachings and practices of our tradition can be profound sources of inspiration, guidance, and support for the work of social justice" (p. xiii).

Taken as a whole, the essays in the book make a convincing case that Jews must address the central social challenges of our time. For the authors, this moral and religious requirement flows primarily from Jewish text and Jewish historical experience, both of which are used creatively and effectively in this anthology. Many of the pieces move beyond a perfunctory use of inspirational one-liners from the tradition—"Justice, justice, shall you pursue"; "You shall not oppress the stranger for you were strangers in the land of Egypt"—and engage in a close reading of a variety of texts that is both inspirational and helpful in finding moral responses to social challenges.

For example, in "Hearing the Voice of the Poor," Aryeh Cohen addresses a dilemma common to large cities: A homeless person is living in a RV parked next to a city playground. The residents are pressuring the police to have the individual forcefully removed. Although he has not hurt anyone, they argue that he is a security risk. They are also clearly concerned that an influx of homeless people to their neighborhood will be unpleasant and lower property values. What would be a Jewish response to this dilemma? To answer this question, Cohen turns to the Mishnah's ruling that residents of a courtyard may force a dissenting homeowner to contribute to the cost of constructing a protective gate. In an interesting twist, the Talmud recounts that Elijah stopped speaking to a Chasid (righteous person) who constructed such a gate. Rashi explains that this was because a fence "gates off the poor people who are shouting [for money or assistance] and their voices are not heard" (p. 141). Cohen notes that responding to or ignoring the cries of those who suffer is a central motif in the Exodus from Egypt. God heard the cries of the Israelites; Pharaoh ignored the cries of the Israelite foremen who complained to him. Cohen's conclusion is powerful:

> If we think about our urban spaces with this fundamental principle in mind—choose to imitate God and not Pharaoh—we inexorably must choose justice over excessive security. We must choose not to hassle the homeless guy in the R.V., even if it may have an impact on our property values. We must choose decriminalizing homelessness over creating a business zone in our downtowns. Above all, we must figure out ways to turn our cars, our ears, and our minds toward the people in the areas of our cities where we do not go. When we are able to hear their cries, we can respond justly (p. 146).

Mark Hanis writes that his efforts to prevent current and future genocides are a direct response to the Holocaust. This is a compelling example of how Jewish history can motivate activism. In *Righteous Indignation* this history is referenced in many contexts. For Judith Rosenbaum, the fact that the first birth control clinic in the United States primarily helped immigrant Jews—the book is full of eye-opening facts such as this—means that Jews should fight for the reproductive rights of today's needy populations. Dara Silverman argues that because Jews have historically both benefited and suffered from America's immigration policies, it is incumbent on us to insure that the country responds generously to this generation's immigrants and refugees. Many of the authors believe that Jews are living at a unique time in our history, one in which many of us enjoy an unprecedented level of social, political, and economic power. This, too, creates responsibility. The Talmud's assertion (BT *Shabbat* 54b) that a person is accountable for all the sins of his household, fellow citizens, and the wider world that she had the power to prevent but did not, is cited to bolster this assertion (p. 291 and elsewhere). Appeals to the lessons and responsibilities that emerge from our historical experience may prove especially resonant with the growing numbers of Jews for whom religion is no longer central to their identities.

As the editors note in the introduction, the general consensus of the contributors to this volume is that the American Jewish community should not prioritize addressing its internal challenges—anti-Semitism, assimilation, cultural continuity, the Jewish poor—over responding to the needs of the wider society. It should address both areas simultaneously. As Ruth Messinger and Aaron Dorfman explain, "All of us are global consumers, purchasing items that have arrived in our stores as a result of transnational economic interconnectedness. And most of us are also global investors" (p. 286). These economic interconnections serve to bring the world "out there" into our homes and undermine the traditional Jewish hierarchy of obligation that assumed that Jews were closer to us than outsiders. In my view, Messinger/Dorfman and others do not sufficiently contend with Judaism's positive sense that all Jews are (immediate) family. We are responsible to cater to the needs of family first and then see to the needs of others. In truth, as Danya Ruttenberg notes, addressing internal Jewish issues often causes you to engage the world at large: "Questions about why not everybody can afford those High Holy Day tickets…lead to other questions about the distribution of wealth in a community, in a city, in America" (p. 209). There is no approach to taking care of Jews who are poor, unemployed, without adequate health care, or being denied same-sex benefits without seeking to change the socioeconomic reality of all people.

Whereas activists like Arthur Waskow often infuse traditional Jewish ritual with specific political content, the other authors featured in this anthology do not seem inclined to follow this path. Ritual, in fact, is rarely mentioned here. When it does appear, its function is more to—as the editors state—"help us sustain ourselves in the face of the suffering and despair we encounter daily in our work" (p. xv), than to give voice to specific political positions. Margie Klein's unique way of staging the Friday night Kiddush (p. 34) has more in common with Alpert's prayers at the abortion clinic than with the Freedom Seder. My students at

McGill generally react negatively to examples of politicized Jewish ritual. Accordingly, I am inclined to see this apparent shift in focus positively.

For both Alpert and the authors of *Righteous Indignation*, developing a progressive politics that references Jewish religious vocabulary, text, and history is essential to countering the influence of the Christian Religious Right. They seem to accept Michael Lerner's view, expressed in his recent book *The Left Hand of God* and elsewhere, that the Left's vocabulary of "rights and economic entitlements" is not sufficient to capture hearts and souls and cannot, therefore, trigger or sustain major efforts to change our world. And these authors want to see a changed world. They are not content with Mitzvah Days and other service-oriented social justice projects that provide necessary and important relief but leave the larger frameworks that cause suffering intact. In the words of Jonah Pesner, "It is time for the Jewish community to begin living out the vision of Isaiah that we read at Yom Kippur each year. Instead of spending one or two days 'donning sackcloth,' we must become the 'repairers of the breach' (58:12) of our social fabric" (p. 89). These books remind us that the Jewish community has the human, financial, and cultural resources necessary to spearhead such a repair.

ERIC CAPLAN is the author of *From Ideology to Liturgy: Reconstructionist Worship and American Liberal Judaism* (Cincinnati: Hebrew Union College Press, 2002). He is associate professor and chair of the Department of Jewish Studies and director of the Jewish Teacher Training Program at McGill University in Montreal.

Drawing in the Dust
Zoë Klein
(New York: Pocket Books, 2009), 360 pp.

In Jeremiah 16, God tells the prophet, "You are not to marry and not to have sons and daughters in this place." Uncharacteristically for a man of his time, Jeremiah indeed remained unmarried. Yet, like Hosea before him, he used the imagery of married love to express the relationship between God and Israel. Abraham Joshua Heschel makes a case for Jeremiah's self-perception as God's celibate bride.[1] However, an aggadah in *Bava Kama* 16b paints Jeremiah as a sexual being, whom the people maliciously accused of illicit relations. Because another midrash traces Jeremiah's lineage through Rahab, his proclivity for harlots—and therefore the possibility of his not being celibate—was apparently established in the Rabbinic mind.

Jeremiah's divinely imposed bachelorhood (no other prophet was forbidden to marry) and the discomfort it raises provided Zoë Klein the seed for her wonderfully inventive novel in which she explores the possibility of Anatiya, the handmaiden cum prophetess, who loves Jeremiah from afar and late in life becomes his lover.

Unlike Anita Diamant's *The Red Tent*, which brought us directly into a contemporaneous biblical world, *Drawing in the Dust* remains fully ensconced in the twenty-first century. We never actually meet Anatiya or Jeremiah in real time. We are introduced to them only through their writings and the imaginings of the novel's characters. The protagonist, Page Brookstone, is an American-born Catholic archaeologist living in Israel whose historic find of artifacts related to the prophet Jeremiah includes cistern paintings of his life and the exile, Anatiya's scroll, and the coffin in which Jeremiah and Anatiya's skeletons are found embracing for eternity.

The modern story is a page-turner, filled with intrigue about Arab-Israeli relations (the dig takes place under the home of an Arab couple in modern day Anatot, Jeremiah's home town), secular academic politicking (due to fear of ultra-Orthodox backlash regarding new archaeological proof of Jeremiah's authorship of Deuteronomy), actual ultra-Orthodox backlash against the desecration of Jeremiah's grave, and a Christian fundamentalist plot to bring Armageddon. It is also a love story in and of itself, the publicized love story of Jeremiah and Anatiya creates an epidemic of love throughout the world and forever changes the trajectory of Page's life.

But the real gift of Zoë Klein's novel is Anatiya's scroll itself. One is sure to be tantalized by the snippets in *Drawing in the Dust* and will therefore be delighted to know that the fictional scroll is available in its entirety as a separate book entitled *The Scroll of Anatiya*.[2] Its fifty-two chapters, written in beautiful lyrical language in a biblical style that plays off of the fifty-two chapters of the book of Jeremiah, rivals the Song of Songs as a text of longing, desire, and ultimate consummation. But it is also a testament to Jeremiah's suffering from an outsider's perspective.

Anatiya's is a parallel experience to that of Jeremiah. When he says at his commissioning (Jer. 1), "I don't know how to speak," Anatiya herself becomes mute for life, writing "When God put out a hand and touched your mouth, God put out another hand and touched the tip of a finger to my lips, whispering, 'shhh'..." (*Drawing in the Dust*, p. 194). When God famously sends Jeremiah to study the work of the potter (Jer. 18), Anatiya's chapter 18 brings us the words of the potter himself: "If you have no respect for the void and its immense power...then you cannot understand (p. 95)."

The novel implies that Jeremiah's metaphors are not all his own, that they come to him through his interactions with Anatiya. His reference in Jeremiah 1:13 to a steaming pot as a metaphor for the lands to the north is a reference in Anatiya's parallel verse "to an actual steaming pot with which she cooks" for him (p. 196). Page therefore asserts, "Wherever he is metaphorical, she is literal," speculating that Jeremiah could "have been watching her and drawing his metaphors from her."

The novel and the scroll thereby provide wonderful lessons in intertextuality. As Page is about to notate for academic posterity that Anatiya's verse "I lie awake on my couch" is a reference to Song of Songs, she hesitates, reflecting, "Who is to say whether the phrase originated with an outside source or with Anatiya herself? Who is to say that Jeremiah, Proverbs, the Song of Songs, and Job aren't all quoting her?" (p. 195). Recognizable verses from these and other biblical texts find their way into Anatiya's prose and thrill the knowledgeable Bible reader.

We are in the fortunate position of having more authentic information about Jeremiah than about any other Hebrew prophet. Not only is his book one of the longest in Tanach, containing a considerable amount of biographical information (preserved by his scribe Baruch), but also a number of passages often referred to as Jeremiah's "confessions" vividly reveal his inner life, including outcries and prayers and a few of God's responses, as well. Nonetheless, through Anatiya's fictional writings, which both headline each chapter of *Drawing in the Dust* and are later interspersed in the fictional narrative, we are presented with the possibility of an even fuller emotional and experiential range for our beleaguered prophet. Yes, Anatiya's scroll paints the picture we already have in our minds of the divine burden Jeremiah carries, his public rejection, the inner tension between his natural inclination toward introspection and his deep sense of vocation and loyalty. But we also entertain the possibility that he was loved by a woman who suffered with him and for him, whose own life mirrored his own, and whose metaphors become part of his prophecies.

Elie Wiesel writes of Jeremiah that, "there was no joy in his life, ever. No pleasant surprises, no warmth, no smiles; nothing but sorrow, anguish and tears. Words of woe and anger—words he was made to speak against his will. He wanted to speak of other things; he wanted to be a normal person dealing with customary human problems and not with eternity and death, but he had no choice."[3]

Zoë Klein gave Jeremiah that choice in *Drawing in the Dust*, in which joy, pleasant surprises, and a person named Jeremiah dealing with customary human problems like love can exist. While the speed with which the archaeological dig and the translation of the scroll unfolds defies credibility, straining the reader's suspension of disbelief, the delight provided by Anatiya's scroll itself are well-worth these shortcomings of the contemporary narrative.

The novel spoon-feeds the reader some of the connections between the book of Jeremiah and Anatiya's scroll, but the real thrill of the hunt is in trying to find one's own connections, moving back and forth from Anatiya's text to the Book of Jeremiah. Close readers of Jeremiah will search for the clues that Rabbi Klein herself may have found therein to inspire Anatiya's writings. Where Anatiya writes in chapter 22, "If you were a signet ring upon my right hand, I would press you into the wax and seal each of my scrolls with your sign," Jeremiah 22:24 quotes God angrily telling the king, "If you were a signet on my right hand, I would tear you off even from there." When God commands Jeremiah to make and wear a yoke on his neck (Jer. 27:2), Anatiya writes (in her own chapter 27), "If I could spirit that yoke away... but God guards you so tightly" (p. 150).

The possibilities for creative adult education abound, both to inspire a deeper appreciation of our great prophet Jeremiah as well as to teach about themes such as intertextuality, urtexts, or contemporary midrash. Themes and images from Jeremiah's prophecy take on new significance through Rabbi Klein's rereading. She does a remarkable job of bringing Jeremiah to life in new ways, of expanding the boundaries of our religious imaginations. This includes the astounding assertion that the Jerusalem that Jeremiah wrote about in Lamentations was not a place at all, but was Anatiya herself. Reading the book for that episode alone would be dayeinu, but there is so much more to be grateful for.

Notes

1. Abraham Joshua Heschel, *The Prophets,* vol. I (New York: Harper and Row, 1962), 113–15.
2. Zoë Klein, *The Scroll of Anatiya*, Eugene, OR (Resource Publications, 2009), 177 pp.
3. Elie Wiesel, *Five Biblical Portraits* (University of Notre Dame Press, 1981), 103.

RABBI PAMELA WAX (NY94), the staff rabbi and spiritual care coordinator at Westchester Jewish Community Services, runs the WJCS Jewish Healing Center.

From Rebel to Rabbi: Reclaiming Jesus and the Making of Modern Jewish Culture
by Matthew Hoffman
(Stanford, CA: Stanford University Press, 2007), 292 pp.

The figure of Jesus has challenged and intrigued Jews since the very beginning of Christianity. The Gospel writers either were Jews themselves or relied on sources originally compiled by Jews; Paul struggled to reconcile his Jewishness with his faith in the risen Christ. As Christianity and Judaism developed separate identities in late antiquity, and especially as the Church became the political power dominating Jewish life in medieval Europe, Jews by necessity developed ways of understanding Jesus that provided a compelling counter-narrative to the dominant Christian one. Jews came to see Jesus not as the fulfillment of biblical prophecy and the path to salvation but rather as representing the latest incarnation of a long line of implacable enemies, from Pharaoh to Balaam to Titus. With the rise of modernity, however, this negative caricature of Jesus ceased to be an effective strategy for Jews navigating the challenges and opportunities of a world no longer dominated by the church. A new, more positive assessment of Jesus the Jew (though not necessarily of the Christian Christ) emerged in Jewish scholarly and literary circles, provoking controversy and fierce debate within the Jewish community.

Many scholars have written about Jewish views of Jesus in the modern era.[1] Matthew Hoffman's *From Rebel to Rabbi* differs from these treatments in both approach and scope. While others scholars have concentrated almost exclusively on the writings of Western European and American scholars, philosophers, and rabbis, Hoffman widens his lens to include the fields of Yiddish and Hebrew literature and art, whose flourishing between the 1860s and the 1940s among Eastern European Jews was as essential to the evolution of modern Jewish identity—especially secular identity—as the fields of critical scholarship and theology. Other writers have tended to foreground the different images of Jesus as their primary subject; Hoffman is more interested in what theses images reveal about Jews themselves:

> By focusing on changing Jewish approaches to the figure of Jesus we can lay bare the process by which Jews created modern alternatives to traditional modes of Jewish identity, thought, and culture. In this sense, I argue that the "Jewish question"—how do modern Jews relate to the figure of Jesus?—is really a microcosm of the "Jewish question"—how do modern Jews define themselves in relation to the non-Jewish environment? (p. 3)

In his first chapter, Hoffman examines the Jewish counterpart of the nineteenth century Protestant quest for the historical Jesus. Jewish historians and reformers, informed by Enlightenment values and biblical scholarship, and responding to changing social and political realities, abandoned the unflattering portrayals of Jesus found in Rabbinic and medieval literature and "reclaimed" him as a Jew. This Jewish Jesus, whether a "rabbi, an Essene, or a prophet" (p. 7) offered Western European Jews an alternative to both the traditional Jewish and Christian views of Jesus that "conformed to and even bolstered" (p. 8) the new models of Jewish identity they were formulating in response to modernity.

In the second chapter, Hoffman shifts his attention to Eastern Europe, where the Jewish enlightenment and the Jewish reclamation of Jesus occurred in a very different political and social environment than in the West, including the influences of Zionism and socialism. As they strove to craft a secular Jewish identity, Yiddish and Hebrew writers and artists engaged in wide-ranging, heated debates over the appropriate Jewish stance regarding the figure of Jesus, who often represented Western culture as a whole. Competing strategies and ideologies crystallized around particular approaches to the "Jesus question." As examples, Hoffman discusses two such clashes that consumed Yiddish and Hebrew literature between 1909 and 1913: the "Crucifix question" that roiled around the Yiddish authors S. Ansky (1863–1920) and Chaim Zhitlovsky (1865–1943) and the Brenner Affair at the center of which were the Hebrew writers Ahad Ha'am (1856–1927) and Yosef Chaim Brenner (1881–1921).

Having enumerated core questions and the range of views surrounding the Jewish reclamation of Jesus in both Western and Eastern Europe, Hoffman devotes the rest of his book to "images of Jesus, Christ-like figures, and Christian symbolism in modernist Yiddish texts and works of art" (p. 8). In a paragraph that succinctly sums up his thesis, Hoffman writes,

> For such writers and artists as Sholem Asch, Uri Tsvi Grinberg, and Marc Chagall, refiguring Jesus and using Christological themes to express aspects of the modern Jewish experience were an integral part of creating a new and distinctive modern Jewish culture. Their rebellion against the theological-religious essence of Judaism included the creation of a Jewish Jesus that unhinged the figure of Jesus from his Christian theological moorings and allowed him to be part of an emerging secular Jewish discourse. The Jewish writers and artists [...] were no longer solely interested in Jesus as a historical or theological figure; they became primarily fascinated by the image of the crucified Jesus for the symbolic meaning it could bring to their work as an emblem of martyrdom, failed redemption, tragedy, and suffering, both Jewish and universal. It was part of the modernist penchant for cultural hybridity and symbolic syncretism that was at the center of creating secular Jewish culture. However, in many ways, the central components of the reclamation of Jesus in the German Haskalah and Reform movements also permeated the portrayals of Jesus in Yiddish literature and the visual arts. For many Jewish writers and artists, the Jewish Jesus they created was a weapon against Christian anti-Semitism and cultural dominance; it served as a polemical thrust against Western-Christian culture by depicting Jesus as an inherently Jewish symbol, and the Jews as the quintessential Christ-like victims of Christian violence and persecution. (p. 9)

Hoffman's detailed and meticulous research ranges over Hebrew, Yiddish, and Russian literature, as well as modernist painting, and he effectively uses the insights of contemporary critical theory as he develops his analysis. By including these works, he goes beyond many of his predecessors in chronicling the modern Jewish engagement with Jesus. Hoffman demonstrates that, for a broad spectrum of Jews in the late nineteenth and early twentieth centuries, coming to terms with the figure of Jesus, however differently imagined, was synonymous with coming to terms with modernity and essential to modern secular constructions of Jewish identity. The figure of Jesus no longer stirs the same level of passion it did in the era Hoffman examines in *From Rebel to Rabbi*, but it remains a potent symbol for the culture in which many Jews continue to live and therefore one with which they still have to contend.

Notes

1. See, for example, Shalom Ben Chorin, "The Image of Jesus in Modern Judaism," *Journal of Ecumenical Studies* 11 (1974): 401–30; George L. Berlin, *Defending the Faith: Nineteenth-Century American Jewish Writings on Christianity and Jesus*, SUNY series in religious studies (Albany: State University of New York Press, 1989); Beatrice Butreau, ed., *Jesus through Jewish Eyes: Rabbis and Scholars Engage an Ancient Brother in a New Conversation* (Maryknoll, NY: Orbis Press, 2001); David R. Catchpole, *The Trial of Jesus: A Study in the Gospels and Jewish Historiography from 1770 to the Present Day*, Studia post-Biblica, v. 18 (Leiden: E. J. Brill, 1971); J. S. Connong, "The Changing Attitude of Jews to Jesus," *Union Seminary Review* 48 (1936–37): 323–32; Herbert Danby, *The Jews and Christianity* (London: Sheldon, 1927); Walter Jacob, *Christianity through Jewish Eyes: The Quest for Common Ground* (Cincinnati: Hebrew Union College Press, 1974); Joseph Klausner, *Jesus of Nazareth*, trans. Herbert Danby (New York: Macmillan, 1925), 106–24; Gösta Lindeskog, *Die Jesusfrage in Neuzeitlichen Judentum* (Uppsala: Almquist & Wiksells, 1938); Samuel Sandmel, "The Jewish Scholar and Early Christianity," in *The Seventy-Fifth Anniversary Volume of the Jewish Quarterly Review*, ed. Abraham A. Newman and Solomon Zeitlin (New York: Ktav, 1967), 473–81; Samuel Sandmel, *A Jewish Understanding of the New Testament* (Woodstock, VT: Skylight Paths, 2005). E. S. Tanner, "Recent Jewish Interpretations of Jesus," *Journal of Biblical Literature* 8 (1940): 80–82; T. Walker, *Jewish Views of Jesus* (New York: Macmillan, 1931); Walter P Weaver, *The Historical Jesus in the Twentieth Century, 1900–1950* (Harrisburg, PA: Trinity

International Press, 1999), 230–56; Trude Weiss-Rosmarin, *Jewish Expressions on Jesus: An Anthology* (New York: Ktav, 1977).

DAVID FOX SANDMEL (C83) is Crown-Ryan Associate Professor of Jewish Studies, Catholic Theological Union and Director of Lifelong Learning, Temple Sholom of Chicago.

The CCAR Journal: The Reform Jewish Quarterly
Published quarterly by the Central Conference of American Rabbis.

Volume LVII, No. 1. Issue Number: Two hundred twenty-three.
Winter 2010.

STATEMENT OF PURPOSE

The CCAR Journal: The Reform Jewish Quarterly seeks to explore ideas and issues of Judaism and Jewish life, primarily—but not exclusively—from a Reform Jewish perspective. To fulfill this objective, the Journal is designed to:

1. provide a forum to reflect the thinking of informed and concerned individuals—especially Reform rabbis—on issues of consequence to the Jewish people and the Reform Movement;

2. increase awareness of developments taking place in fields of Jewish scholarship and the practical rabbinate, and to make additional contributions to these areas of study;

3. encourage creative and innovative approaches to Jewish thought and practice, based upon a thorough understanding of the traditional sources.

The views expressed in the Journal do not necessarily reflect the position of the Editorial Board or the Central Conference of American Rabbis.

The CCAR Journal: The Reform Jewish Quarterly (ISSN 1058-8760) is published quarterly by the Central Conference of American Rabbis, 355 Lexington Avenue, 18th Floor, New York, NY, 10017. Application to mail at periodical postage rates is pending at New York, NY and at additional mailing offices.

Subscriptions should be sent to CCAR Executive Offices, 355 Lexington Avenue, 18th Floor, New York, NY, 10017. Subscription rate as set by the Conference is $75 for a one-year subscription, $125 for a two-year subscription. Overseas subscribers should add $36 per year for postage. POSTMASTER: Please send address changes to The CCAR Journal: The Reform Jewish Quarterly, c/o Central Conference of American Rabbis, 355 Lexington Avenue, 18th Floor, New York, NY, 10017.

Typesetting and publishing services provided by Publishing Synthesis, Ltd., 39 Crosby Street, New York, NY, 10013.

The CCAR Journal: The Reform Jewish Quarterly is indexed in the *Index to Jewish Periodicals*. Articles appearing in it are listed in the *Index of Articles on Jewish Studies* (of *Kirjath Sepher*).

© Copyright 2010 by the Central Conference of American Rabbis.
All rights reserved.
ISSN 1058-8760

ISBN: 978-0-88123-157-1

GUIDELINES FOR SUBMITTING MATERIAL

1. The *CCAR Journal* welcomes submissions that fulfill its Statement of Purpose whatever the author's background or identification. Inquiries regarding publishing in the CCAR Journal and submissions for possible publication (including poetry) should be sent to the editor, Rabbi Susan Laemmle, in electronic form via <u>Laemmle@usc.edu</u>. Should problems arise, call 323-939-4084.

2. Other than commissioned articles, submissions to the *CCAR Journal* are sent out to a member of the editorial board for anonymous peer review. Thus submitted articles and poems should be sent to the editor with the author's name omitted. Please use MS Word format for the attachment. The message itself should contain the author's name, phone number, and e-mail address, as well as the submission's title and a 1–2 sentence bio.

3. Based on Reform Judaism's commitment to egalitarianism, we request that articles be written in gender-inclusive language.

4. Books for review and inquiries regarding submitting a review should be sent directly to the book review editor, Rabbi Laurence Edwards, at <u>Laurenceedwards@sbcglobal.net</u>.

5. The *Journal* publishes reference notes at the end of articles, but submissions are easier to review when notes come at the bottom of each page. If possible, keep this in mind when submitting an article. Notes should conform to the following style:

   a. Norman Lamm, *The Shema: Spirituality and Law in Judaism* (Philadelphia: Jewish Publication Society, 1998), 101–6. **[book]**

   b. Lawrence A. Hoffman, "The Liturgical Message," in *Gates of Understanding*, ed. Lawrence A.Hoffman (New York: CCAR Press, 1977), 147–48, 162–63. **[chapter in a book]**

   c. Richard Levy, "The God Puzzle," *Reform Judaism* 28 (Spring 2000): 18–22. **[article in a periodical]**

   d. Lamm, *Shema*, 102. **[short form for subsequent reference]**

   e. Levy, "God Puzzle," 20. **[short form for subsequent reference]**

   f. Ibid., 21. **[short form for subsequent reference]**

6. If Hebrew script is used, please include an English translation. If transliteration is used, follow the guidelines abbreviated below and included more fully in the **Master Style Sheet**, available on the CCAR website at <u>www.ccarnet.org</u>:

   "ch" for *chet* and *chaf*   "ei" for *tzeirei*
   "f" for *fei*   "a" for *patach* and *kamatz*
   "k" for *kaf* and *kuf*   "o" for *cholam* and *kamatz katan*
   "tz" for *tzadi*   "u" for *shuruk* and *kibbutz*
   "i" for *chirik*   "ai" for *patach* with *yod*
   "e" for *segol*

   Final "h" for final *hei*; none for final *ayin* (with exceptions based on common usage): *atah*, *Sh'ma*, <u>but</u> *Moshe*.

   Apostrophe for *sh'va nah*: *b'nei*, *b'rit*, *Sh'ma*; no apostrophe for *sh'va nach*.

   Hyphen for two vowels together where necessary for correct pronunciation: *ne-eman*, *samei-ach*, <u>but</u> *maariv*, Shavuot.

   No hyphen for prefixes unless necessary for correct pronunciation: *babayit*, HaShem, Yom HaAtzma-ut.

   Do not double consonants (with exceptions based on dictionary spelling or common usage): *t'filah*, *chayim*, <u>but</u> *tikkun*, Sukkot.

www.ingramcontent.com/pod-product-compliance
Lightning Source LLC
Chambersburg PA
CBHW050636160426
43194CB00010B/1696